# Justice Calls

# Justice Calls

SERMONS OF WELCOME
AND AFFIRMATION

※

*edited by*
PHIL SNIDER

CASCADE *Books* • Eugene, Oregon

JUSTICE CALLS
Sermons of Welcome and Affirmation

Copyright © 2016 Wipf and Stock Publishers. All rights reserved. Except for brief quotations in critical publications or reviews, no part of this book may be reproduced in any manner without prior written permission from the publisher. Write: Permissions, Wipf and Stock Publishers, 199 W. 8th Ave., Suite 3, Eugene, OR 97401.

Cascade Books
An Imprint of Wipf and Stock Publishers
199 W. 8th Ave., Suite 3
Eugene, OR 97401

www.wipfandstock.com

ISBN 13: 978-1-4982-0201-5

HB ISBN 13: 978-1-4982-8842-2

*Cataloging-in-Publication data:*

Justice calls : sermons of welcome and affirmation / edited by Phil Snider.

xx + 172 p. ; 23 cm. —Includes bibliographical references.

ISBN 13: 978-1-4982-0201-5

1. Homosexuality—Religious aspects—Christianity. 2. Preaching. I. Snider, Phil, 1973–.

BR115.H6 S65 2016

Manufactured in the U.S.A.

Bible quotations, unless otherwise noted, are from the New Revised Standard Version Bible, copyright © 1989, Division of Christian Education of the National Council of the Churches of Christ in the United States of America. Used by permission. All rights reserved.

Scripture quotations marked (CEB) are taken from the Common English Bible. Copyright © 2011 by Common English Bible.

Scripture quotations marked (NIV) are taken from the Holy Bible, New International Version®, NIV®. Copyright © 1973, 1978, 1984, 2011 by Biblica Inc.™ Used by permission of Zondervan. All rights reserved worldwide. www.zondervan.com.

Details in some anecdotes and stories have been changed to protect the identities of the persons involved.

*For all who've been excluded by the church because of who they love*

I don't believe in the godliness of steeples,
but I believe in the stained glass.

—ANDREA GIBSON

# Contents

*Acknowledgments xi*
*List of Contributors xiii*
*Introduction by Phil Snider xv*

PART ONE: Calling for Equality

1. The Rule of Love  3
*1 John 4:7–21*
Carol Howard Merritt

2. The Pearl of Great Price  7
*Matthew 13:45–46*
Monica A. Coleman

3. The Biblical Support for Same-Sex Marriage  12
*Genesis 2:18*
Rita Nakashima Brock

4. Descriptive or Definitive?  18
*Romans 6:3–4; 8:14–17*
David J. Lose

5. Looking for Love  23
*Genesis 24:34–38, 42–49, 58–67*
*Song of Songs 2:8–13*
W. Scott Haldeman

6. Deeper than Biology  30
*Genesis 2:18–25*
Barbara K. Lundblad

# Contents

## PART TWO: Calling for Liberation

7. Whosoever  37
*John 3:16*
ALTON B. POLLARD III

8. I Think That's What It Takes  44
*Matthew 22:1–14*
DEREK PENWELL

9. It's Harder to Be Us: The Gospel of Forgiveness for People on the Margins  50
*John 20:19–31*
SANDHYA RANI JHA

10. In Memory of Brandy Martell  56
*Hebrews 12:1–3*
*Ephesians 6:10–18*
TAI AMRI SPANN-WILSON

11. All of You  60
*Romans 12:2*
MEREDITH GUEST

12. Dogs of Canaan  66
*Matthew 15:21–28*
CHRISTIAN PIATT

## PART THREE: Calling for Hospitality

13. All Are Welcome?  75
*Luke 4:16–32*
NANCY STEEVES

14. The Doctrine of Original Fabulousness  79
*John 13:33–35*
STEPHANIE SPELLERS

15. Water on a Desert Road  83
*Isaiah 56:1–8*
*Acts 8:26–40*
BARBARA K. LUNDBLAD

## Contents

16. A Divine Flame  88
*Song of Songs 2:16—3:4; 8:6–7*
DEBORAH A. APPLER

17. Luke's Stonewall  94
*Luke 7:36–50*
MONA WEST

18. Healing Our -isms  98
*Ephesians 2:11–22*
IRENE MONROE

19. The Storm Is Passing Over  105
*1 Samuel 17*
*Mark 4:35–41*
MARY FOULKE

PART FOUR: Calling for Transformation

20. A Queer Eye for the Straight Bible Reader  113
*Genesis 19:1–11*
MIGUEL A. DE LA TORRE

21. The Bible Says It . . . I Believe It . . . That Settles It?  121
*Ephesians 4:1–16*
GLEN MILES

22. The Coherent and the Contingent  128
*Leviticus 18:22; 20:8–18*
*1 Corinthians 7:10–15*
ERIC ELNES

23. Text and Taboo  135
*Acts 10:1–33*
TAD DELAY

24. Rolling Back the Stone  139
*John 20:19–23*
HOLLY E. HEARON

## Contents

25. Why I Changed My Mind on Homosexuality  146
*Romans 1*
DANNY CORTEZ

26. Picking Up the Mantle  162
*2 Kings 2:1–14*
RICHARD F. WARD

*For Further Reading*  169
*Bibliography*  171

# Acknowledgments

There are debts I owe to others that I cannot begin to repay.

This book is the product of an incredible group of contributors with a heart for justice and equality. Their vision, courage, and commitment is exemplary. Having the opportunity to collaborate with each of them has been one of the deepest joys of my vocational life. Words are not enough to express my thanks to each of you.

I'm also exceedingly grateful for those I've worked with through the Center for Diversity and Reconciliation at Brentwood Christian Church, as well as Brieta Self, whose behind-the-scenes work at Brentwood helps make so many things possible. The collegiality and friendship extended to me by Charlie Bahn, Emily Bowen-Marler, Chad Mattingly, Micki Pulleyking, and Darryl Schafer is immeasurable. I'd like to thank Stephanie Perkins and everyone at PROMO, who tirelessly work for dignity and equality for all people in Missouri (and who have supported me at every turn), as well as Jeff and Kathy Munzinger with PFLAG and Mark Johnston with GLAD. You are part of the work that is saving the world.

To my (nearly) lifelong friends David Boyd and Randy Cathcart, thank you. We aren't as young as we once were, but perhaps our vision is getting better with age. Thanks also to Bob and Cindy Stephens for helping transcribe sermons for this book, and to Brad Lyons and Steve Knight in helping with the formation of this project.

I'm pleased to again be working with the good people at Wipf and Stock on this publication, and I'd like to thank them for making this book a reality.

As always, I reserve my deepest thanks for my parents, Terry and Ann, as well as my wife, Amanda, and our three children, Eli, Sam, and Lily Grace. I find great promise in the fact that my kids don't understand why

## Acknowledgments

publishing this book is so important to me. To them, affirming LGBTQ people is part of what it means to be a Christian, and they don't realize the extent to which churches have struggled with this for so long. As my fourteen-year-old son once said, "You mean there are churches that don't accept people because they are gay? That can't be right." With words such as these, I'm hopeful that the church is moving forward.

Phil Snider
October 12, 2015

# Contributors

**Deborah A. Appler**, Associate Professor of Old Testament/Hebrew Bible at Moravian Theological Seminary.

**Rita Nakashima Brock**, Research Professor in Theology and Culture and Director of the Soul Repair Center at Brite Divinity School.

**Monica A. Coleman**, Associate Professor of Constructive Theology and African American Religions at Claremont School of Theology.

**Danny Cortez**, pastor of New Heart Community Church in La Mirada, California.

**Miguel A. De La Torre**, Professor of Social Ethics and Latino/a Studies at Iliff School of Theology.

**Tad DeLay**, PhD student studying philosophy of religion at Claremont School of Theology.

**Eric Elnes**, pastor of Countryside Community Church in Omaha, Nebraska.

**Mary Foulke**, rector of St. Mary's Episcopal Church, Manhattanville, in New York City.

**Meredith Guest**, author of the memoir, *Son, I Like Your Dress*.

**W. Scott Haldeman**, Associate Professor of Worship at Chicago Theological Seminary.

CONTRIBUTORS

**Holly E. Hearon**, T. J. and Virginia Liggett Professor of Christian Traditions and Professor of New Testament Emerita at Christian Theological Seminary.

**Sandhya Rani Jha**, Director of the Oakland Peace Center in Oakland, California.

**David J. Lose**, President of the Lutheran Theological Seminary at Philadelphia.

**Barbara K. Lundblad**, Joe R. Engle Professor of Preaching Emerita at Union Theological Seminary in the City of New York.

**Carol Howard Merritt**, award-winning author and speaker, and cohost (with Derrick Weston) of *God Complex Radio*.

**Glen Miles**, pastor of Country Club Christian Church (Disciples of Christ) in Kansas City, Missouri.

**Irene Monroe**, *Huffington Post* blogger and syndicated religion columnist.

**Derek Penwell**, pastor of Douglass Boulevard Christian Church (Disciples of Christ) in Louisville, Kentucky.

**Christian Piatt**, writer, speaker, editor, and spoken-word artist.

**Alton B. Pollard III**, Dean and Professor of Religion and Culture at Howard University School of Divinity.

**Tai Amri Spann-Wilson**, poet, teacher, and community organizer in Oakland, California.

**Stephanie Spellers**, Canon for Missional Vitality in the Diocese of Long Island.

**Nancy Steeves**, Minister of Southminster-Steinhauer United Church in Edmonton, Alberta.

**Richard F. Ward**, Fred B. Craddock Professor of Homiletics and Worship at Phillips Theological Seminary.

**Mona West**, Director of the Office of Formation and Leadership Development for the Metropolitan Community Churches.

# Introduction

> My own view is that the outcome of a careful debate about these matters would be to show that there simply are no arguments to show that homosexual love is of itself anything else than love, and that therefore, since the essence of the Torah is love, it hardly falls afoul of the law. To be sure, when it is not love, when it is promiscuity, or infidelity to a sworn partner, or rape, or the sexual abuse of minors, or in any way violent, then it is indeed not love, but that is no less true of heterosexuality.
>
> —John D. Caputo[1]

This book was put together for those with whom we've wept—those who, because of their sexual orientation or gender identity, have been hurt or denied a place in the churches for far too long. Those of us who contributed to this book have had our collective hearts broken on countless occasions as we've listened to friends share stories of rejection, exclusion, and sorrow. We long for people to know there are generous, welcoming, and affirming approaches to Christianity that are deeply rooted in the Bible and are very much alive in the churches, if only one knows where to look.

At the same time, this book was also put together for those who wonder if their faith can allow them to be welcoming and affirming of their lesbian, gay, bisexual, transgender, or queer/questioning (LGBTQ) family members, friends, and neighbors. Is it possible to take the Bible seriously, with authority, and not have to believe that homosexuality is the kind of sin we've often been conditioned or taught to think it is?

Not long ago, a pastor friend of mine told me she met with a member of her church named Andrew, along with his parents, on his twenty-first

---

1. Caputo, *What Would Jesus Deconstruct?*, 110.

INTRODUCTION

birthday. Andrew had just come out to his mom and dad a few weeks before, and even though they desperately wanted to be able to accept him for who he was, they had been taught by their church that simply wasn't possible. As much as they wanted to, the teachings of their church wouldn't allow them to affirm the truth about their son—that he was a gay man, that this was a central part of his identity, and that he didn't choose his sexual orientation any more than they had chosen theirs. When Andrew's parents asked him what he wanted as a birthday present, he asked only that they get together for a conversation with his pastor and him on his birthday, which is what prompted this meeting. More than anything, Andrew wanted his parents to know that he didn't have to deny his religious convictions in order to accept the truth about his sexuality, and they didn't have to disregard the Bible in order to fully accept him.

It is my hope that the sermons in this book can function in a similar way—to help LGBTQ people know they don't have to deny their religious convictions in order to celebrate and accept the truth about their sexuality and/or gender identity; and for people of faith to know they don't have to disregard the Bible in order to fully accept and celebrate their LGBTQ friends and family members. I also hope this book encourages people of faith to stand in solidarity with the LGBTQ community, serving as a rich resource to help pastors and churches consider creative ways to speak in the name of love and compassion (including from the pulpit but not limited to it), as well as to reflect on how all Christians—clergy and laity alike—can courageously share and embody good news in a world that is in desperate need of experiencing it. As the local PFLAG chapter's roadside billboards succinctly remind the community in which I live, "Someone you know and love is gay"—and the way the church responds—the way we as individuals respond—can mean the difference between life and death, sometimes figuratively yet other times quite literally.[2]

If I had been told several years ago that I would be editing a collection of sermons that are welcoming and affirming of LGBTQ people, I would have been among the first to object. Most people assume (based in large part on my writings, along with the fifteen minutes of fame I experienced after one of my speeches on LGBTQ rights went viral)[3] that I have always been an advocate for LGBTQ inclusion and equality. But the truth of the matter is that at one point along the way I wasn't open and affirming of

---

2. PFLAG stands for Parents, Families and Friends of Lesbians and Gays.
3. http://www.youtube.com/watch?v=A8JsRx2lois.

## INTRODUCTION

LGBTQ people, mostly because I didn't think my faith as a Christian allowed me to be so. However, over the course of several years my heart and mind have changed, for biblical and experiential reasons that are deeply grounded in Christian theology. The sermons in this collection do a wonderful job of encapsulating several of the reasons why.[4]

It's unfortunate that Christians who are open and affirming of the LGBTQ community have often been accused of not taking the Bible seriously or of rejecting the Bible altogether in order to assimilate to a culture that

---

4. Of course, as a straight cisgender (a term that refers to one who easily identifies with the gender assigned to them at birth) white male, it's important for me to acknowledge there are still all kinds of privileges that people like me simply take for granted. It has taken many years for me to begin to wake up to these realities and to recognize my complicity in systems of exploitation and oppression (related not just to sexual orientation and gender identity but also to race, sexism, etc.), even in the midst of advocating for people who don't identify as a straight white cisgender male. The privileges that I share as a straight cisgender white male in many ways have the accompanying power of Tolkien's ring. And even though on these pages I am quite willing to engage in meaningful conversations related to these dynamics, all of the greatest rhetoric in the world is a far cry from being willing to undergo the kind of event that would lead to transformative change and justice on behalf of all people. In other words, it's much easier for me to talk about the need for justice than it is to actually give up the social privileges and power that come with being a straight cisgender white male. So in a very important way the sermons in this book serve as a sort of prayer for people like me to actually be willing to undergo significant transformation, as opposed to simply taking part in an empty rhetorical gesture that might make one feel better about oneself but in the end just provides a false sense of bravado, a move that would mostly (and tragically) ensure that the power of right relation, to borrow Carter Heyward's felicitous words, doesn't actually have much of a chance to come into being.

On somewhat related terms, it's also important to point out that any form of exploitation and oppression (including but not limited to those based on race, socioeconomic status, sexual orientation, and gender identity) is problematic, and we should constantly work toward building a better world. But this doesn't necessarily mean that everyone who has experienced discrimination or oppression has experienced it in the same way. This is similar to bell hooks' observation related to the film *Crash*, in which she mentioned that for all its strengths *Crash* didn't adequately delve into the differences in race relations between a variety of different ethnic groups, and that the history of slavery in the U.S. leads to experiences among African Americans that are not necessarily the same as the experiences of, say, Muslims in the U.S. To be sure, all forms of oppression are obviously problematic, and none is acceptable. But the experience of discrimination in the U.S. is not a one-size-fits-all category, and the more we recognize the differences between various forms of discrimination the more we honor those who've experienced discrimination, and the better equipped we are to work toward building a better world that honors the integrity and dignity of all people. Indeed, even the experiences of marginalization and oppression undergone by LGBTQ people do not function the same way for all LGBTQ people, as some of these sermons highlight.

# Introduction

is rapidly changing its attitudes in matters related to human sexuality and gender identity. As the sermons in this book show, this popular caricature is hardly accurate. Indeed, the affirmation, welcome, and good news for LGBTQ people shared by each contributing preacher is announced not in spite of the Bible, but because of the Bible; not in spite of one's faith, but because of one's faith; not in spite of Jesus, but precisely because of Jesus. To paraphrase the words of influential theologian Douglas John Hall, "It's our faith in Christ that makes us more inclusive of others, not less."[5]

The role of the preacher is to put the Bible into the hands of the people, not to take it away. This includes putting it into the hands of lesbian, gay, bisexual, and transgender people who've repeatedly been told that the Bible is the last place to look for comfort, rest, and solidarity (not to mention affirmation and welcome), even though Jesus himself, like them, was condemned, excluded, and marginalized by religious and political authorities whose primary objectives of preserving power and maintaining the status quo seem not to have changed all that much down through the centuries.

The preachers in this volume provide readings of the Bible that celebrate the call for justice and liberation that resounds throughout Scripture. This call is expressed most beautifully and poetically and persuasively in stories of unconditional love, hospitality, mutuality, peace, and compassion—stories that are at the very heart of Jesus' ministry and yet, in an irony of ironies, are so often missing in the churches. The preachers in this volume love the Bible enough to take it seriously, which means they engage the texts in all their depth and complexity. To be sure, not every passage in Scripture is friendly toward the LGBTQ community. For instance, there are a handful of verses in the Bible (six or so) that reflect the cultural perspectives of the contexts in which they were written. Some of these verses might have made sense in one time and place, but that doesn't necessarily mean they make sense in all times and places. One of the ways we honor the Bible—that we show our reverence and respect for it—is by reading it contextually, paying significant attention to social context and location. I won't get into the nuances of these verses right now (we'll let the following sermons do the talking), but suffice it to say that the Bible isn't in the business of providing a single point of view on most, if not all, topics, including homosexuality (which, as we'll see, is a topic that, strictly speaking, doesn't

---

5. See Hall, *Why Christian?*, 146. While each of the sermons in this book is written from a Christian perspective, we celebrate the fact that other religious traditions also make room to welcome and affirm the LGBTQ community.

## INTRODUCTION

even appear in the Bible, mostly because the ancients didn't understand sexual orientation in the way we understand it today). Instead, we are given a multiplicity of perspectives forged in a variety of circumstances.

From this point of view, the Bible is better understood as that which starts a conversation rather than that which ends one. It is a rich resource for all times, and each generation is given the challenge of wrestling with its insights. As much as people wish it were possible to make ethical judgments based on "the plain meaning of the Bible," it simply can't be done, all because there isn't any one "plain meaning of the Bible." In the 1800s, for example, slave owners had specific biblical texts that supported their beliefs (e.g., Col 3:22: "Slaves, obey your earthly masters"), but so did the abolitionists, whose biblical texts were those rooted in love, dignity, respect, justice, and liberation. Fortunately, the latter carried more weight than texts based on fear, violence, greed, and barbarism.

When it comes to interpreting the role of Christianity and the church in relation to human sexuality and gender identity, the contributors in this volume are drawn to texts that are deeply rooted in love, dignity, respect, justice, and liberation. Such interpretations have always represented the church at its best, and the sermons in this volume represent the church at its best as well.

I am thankful that the voices in this book are not alone but are representative of many others in our society that are also welcoming and affirming. It is wonderful to see a rapidly growing group of Christians—evangelical and mainline, young and old, Protestant and Catholic—who are no longer content to remain silent in the face of the injustice, discrimination, exploitation, and marginalization that LGBTQ people experience, but instead are raising their collective voice to respond to the call of justice at the heart of the gospel, to give it hands and feet, so that God's dreams for this world and all its people might become a reality, here and now.[6]

---

6. Readers will note that these sermons were delivered before the United States Supreme Court handed down its historic ruling on marriage equality; as such they reflect the respective contexts in which they were originally presented. Of course, as LGBTQ people (and other marginalized groups) know all too well, new legislation does not immediately do away with old discrimination (consider the way racism is still a reality in the United States, even half a century after Jim Crow laws were repealed). So even as we celebrate wonderful gains, we also recognize that the beauty harbored in the name of justice and equality still calls out to us, for there is always more justice to come and more justice to be done. The call at the heart of justice—the call at the heart of these sermons—is expressed in order to help us more fully live into the dreams of God for this world. This call remains every bit as important today as it did before the Supreme Court's ruling.

## Introduction

The following sermons invite you to reflect on interpretations of the Bible that harbor profound beauty, love, healing, and hope. Not just for those who are lesbian, gay, bisexual, or transgender, but for all of us, for we are in this together, LGBTQSCAI alike.[7] "If one member suffers, all suffer together with it; if one member is honored, all rejoice together with it" (1 Cor 12:26). Gay, straight, trans, and cis, we are the body of Christ, *together*. Perhaps we make up a queer body of Christ, but would Jesus want it any other way?

---

7. Lesbian, Gay, Bisexual, Transgender, Queer/Questioning, Straight, Cisgender, Asexual, Intersexual (or, LGBT+).

*Part One*

Calling for Equality

# 1

## The Rule of Love

### Carol Howard Merritt

The Reverend Carol Howard Merritt, an ordained minister in the Presbyterian Church (USA), is a highly sought-after speaker and an award-winning author whose books include *Tribal Church* and *Reframing Hope*. In addition to contributing to numerous books, websites, magazines, and journals, she facilitates UNCO (short for Unconference), an organization that hosts open-space gatherings where participants support one another while planning for the future of the church. She also cohosts *God Complex Radio* and blogs for *The Christian Century*.

---

*1 John 4:7–21*

I swallowed hard as I stood before the congregation. I leaned into the pulpit and squinted to see the faces because the funeral home had dimmed the lights after the intimate group of people gathered. They sat, poised to hear the liturgies, Scriptures, and stories that would invoke memories and speak a word of resurrection in the midst of death.

I opened my prayer book and looked up again, scanning carefully to take in each countenance. It's important for a pastor to be sensitive to different expressions of grief, so I'm always careful to breathe in the mood and emotions before a funeral service. But my awareness felt more crucial this time; there was intensity to my search.

## Part One: Calling for Equality

I was trying to discern if Bruce had a partner. I looked from one face to the next as my heart ached. I hadn't known Bruce, the man who had died three days earlier. His sister whispered to me a little bit about his sexual orientation moments before the service. She wanted me to know that he was gay, but she warned me that not everyone in the community was comfortable with his sexuality, so I was asked not to mention it.

"Did he have a partner?" I asked her.

"I don't know. He could have. Someone was taking care of him all that time." She shook her head. "I was completely supportive of him being gay, but not everyone in our family was, so we never talked about it."

Not bringing up the sexual acts of a man at his funeral is easy to do, but a person's sexual orientation and relationships are much more than what happens in the bedroom. Bruce's life was made up of an intricate web of love, care, and concern. Bruce had been sick for a long time before he died, and as I stood before the mourners at the funeral home, I looked into each face and wondered, Were you the one who took him to the doctor's office? Were you the one who comforted him when he got his diagnosis? Were you the one who bathed him when he could not do it himself? Were you the one who called hospice? Were you the one who held him as he breathed his last breath?

If Bruce had a partner, I knew that person had not been allowed into the intensive care unit. He might have a legal battle over his home in the days to come. But, most pressing for me, he was being denied the dignity of being named as one who was loved and beloved at the funeral.

The service was over in an hour, but those sixty minutes still haunt me now, a decade later. It felt unfair that our religious and civil communities would be so opposed to a sexual act that we could not recognize a relationship. As I preached, I tried to convey the message of the one who heals the brokenhearted, but I could not utter the name of the one who may have mourned the most. I might have failed to bring the good news that day. How could I have proclaimed the message of God's love in that darkness?

"God is love" (1 John 4:8). This passage in 1 John reminds us that God is not a noun but a verb—a pulsing, emanating emotion. This love moves in and among us, allowing neighbors to treat one another with dignity and respect. Love fetters the body of Christ, binding us to one another and compelling us to work for justice in our society. Love stirs within people, inciting passion and causing them to long for promise and commitment. And love allows for years of flourishing beauty within a covenantal relationship.

The emotion takes so many forms. It is that sideways glance that your lover throws to make your stomach quiver in longing. It is the daily acts of charity, even in a world of violence. And it is caring for someone during his last breaths. In all of these things, we act in the image of God when we act in love. When there is division in the body of Christ, there ought to be one response: love. The sinews of our body are joined together by that patient, humble love that never fails.

We see it when, in the very first rules of community life that were penned by Augustine, he states, "Before all else, beloved, love God and then your neighbor, for these are the chief commandments given to us."[1] In all of our acts, we must be guided by love.

In the great struggles of desegregation, when peaceful protesters were soaked by hoses and attacked by snarling dogs, Martin Luther King admonished the men and women to have the strength and courage to love, even in the midst of brutality. And in this moment, we are called to love again.

Right now, many congregations, churches, and denominational bodies feel crushed as they wrestle with same-gender marriage. With considerable conviction, some claim that we ought to keep to a biblical view of marriage—between one man and one woman. Others, like me, who have seen a warm kindness and love grow between same-gender partners, long to make sure that they can enter into a covenant with God and one another, that they can have families, legal rights, tax benefits, insurance coverage, and access to the intensive care unit.

I worry about the caricature that those who support same-gender marriage have thrown out the Bible, or that we do not consider the Bible to be authoritative in our lives. We know that the Bible's witness to the marital relationship is not so clear-cut; it looks much different than what we recognize as marriage in our culture today. The book is full of polygamy, and in one case of hyper-polygamy, as one king of Israel had a thousand wives and concubines. Arranged marriages happened at wells. A man had sex with his wife's slave so that she might conceive an heir for him. Kings married for political alliances. God commanded a prophet to marry a sex worker. David loved Jonathan "more than any woman."[2] Women were so

---

1. Augustine, *Rule of St. Augustine*, Preface.
2. This paraphrase is based on the NRSV translation of 2 Sam 1:26, which reads, "Your love to me was wonderful, passing the love of women." For other examples mentioned in this paragraph, see 1 Kgs 11:3; Gen 29; Gen 16; Hos 1:2; Deut 25:5–6.

reliant on a husband's income and land ownership to survive that when a husband died, she was to marry his brother. Very few of the relationships in Scripture describe a relationship between one man and one woman in the sense that we imagine.

So now, as we come to this struggle for marriage equality, we must depend on the Scriptures, not as a textbook to describe the exact formula for marriage, but in those instructions on how to love. How can we act in God's image? How can we make sure that love flourishes? How can our lives and the body of Christ be strengthened in this time of division? When there is question, when there is doubt, when there is a fracturing in the body, we must rely on love as our guiding principle.

I think about that moment, scanning those gathered faces, looking for Bruce's partner, and I'm sure that a loving community would not have forced a spouse to hide in the shadows of his partner's death. If we were acting as the body of Christ, we would have acted to heal the brokenhearted. We would have surrounded him, cared for him, embraced him, and shown him love.

As we go out, as we struggle with relationships, community, and our life together, may love be our guiding principle. When we do not know how to respond to an important issue in our society, may love be our guiding principle. As we face divisions in our body, may love be our guiding principle. And as we understand our relationships with one another, as we long to create caring relationships and nurture families, may love always be our guiding principle.

And may the love of God, our Creator, our Sustainer, and our Liberator, be with us all. Amen.

# 2

# The Pearl of Great Price

MONICA A. COLEMAN

As both a scholar and activist, the Reverend Dr. Monica A. Coleman is committed to connecting faith with social justice. She is an ordained elder in the African Methodist Episcopal Church and is currently the Associate Professor of Constructive Theology and African American Religions at Claremont School of Theology. This sermon was preached as the homily during the commitment ceremony for Dr. Coleman's friends Connie and Karen. Connie and Karen live in a state where same-gender marriage is illegal. After fifteen years of partnership, they decided to have a wedding-style event that they referred to as "Celebration and Blessings." They have since become legally married in Washington, DC. They reside in the U.S. South. Connie serves as the pastor of a small, inclusive Christian worshiping community.

---

*Matthew 13:45–46*

For those of us who have been raised in and are familiar with Christian traditions, this is a familiar story. Jesus is telling his disciples and the crowds who have gathered what the kingdom of God is like. The kingdom of God is this ideal *something*. It's called by different names, in both the Bible and by believers for years to come: the reign of God, the kingdom of heaven, the *basileia*, the kin-dom of God, the realm of God, the commonwealth of

God. Because inclusivity is a value for us, I'm going to say the "community of God."

What is the community of God like? Jesus never tells us directly. Instead he tells us parables, these short stories, and he tells many of them, to give us a kaleidoscopic picture of what the community of God is like. Jesus gives us these many colored pieces that we can turn around as through a scope and that together can tell us a bit of what the community of God is like.

It's like a treasure hidden in a field; it's like a net thrown into the sea. It's like a merchant in search of fine pearls who, on finding one pearl of great price, went and sold all of her possessions and bought it.

Let's put this in more contemporary language. The community of God is like a woman who liquidated all her savings, cashed in her 401(k), sold her house at below market value, hocked all her jewelry at the local pawn store, and maxed out her credit cards to buy one diamond ring. Are you kidding me?! Finance guru Suze Orman would lose her mind! Can you hear her now? What about your eight months of emergency savings? What about your retirement plan? Do you even know the interest rate on your credit cards? If this woman called in to Suze Orman's television show, on which Orman tells people if they can afford their particular wish-list item, Orman would say, "Denied! Denied! Denied!" Whether it's the economic situation of March 2009 in the United States or ancient Palestine, this is bad economics!

Yes. The community of God is like a woman who has given up all the things she is supposed to value and care about—because she has found a true gem. Yes, the community of God is like women who seem to have lost their minds and all good sense.

But this is what the community of God is like. It's a crazy ideal. It's something completely the opposite of what we are taught to do. It's the opposite of what society expects will happen. It's the opposite of what institutions require of us. It's the opposite of the safe and comfortable route.

And because it's so different from most of what we see around us, because it's the opposite of the largest and loudest and richest and most powerful voices in our midst, many people have assumed that this community of God—this heaven—cannot be found here on Earth. This must be in some other world, in some other lifetime, in some period after our lives here on Earth. But Jesus suggests something else. He suggests that it's an ideal that we should strive for, and hope for, and work for, in our daily lives. That the community of God is not a place, but rather a way of being in the world, a way theologian Sallie McFague says "is characterized by a reversal of worldly expectations and a reorientation brought about by the unmerited graciousness of God to us."[1] The community of God is living in this opposite way that inverts, or turns on its head, all of our expectations. To live out the community of God is not to reflect things as they are but to live as things ought to be.

And this is how Connie and Karen live. They redefine what it means to be family. They redefine what it means to be church. They redefine what it means to open one's door to all who knock. They take seriously the call to imitate our greatest spiritual leaders. They open their home to us nearly every week so we have a place to worship that is inclusive and progressive and committed to community. They open their table so we can rest and eat and share our stories together. They open their hearts, literally linking their daily lives and joys and frustrations with those of others around them. Their life together—or rather their love together—has become one of the many colored fragments that we can lift up and look through to see a bit of how we all ought to be.

And I imagine that this is not what they envisioned over fifteen years ago when they fell in love. I imagine that they only knew that they had found in one another a true gem.

But this is actually why we have weddings, right? Because love, by its very nature, is a private affair. Only Karen and Connie know the intricate details of their relationship. Only they know their impressions the first time they met. Only they know the surge they felt when they first kissed. Only they know how everything seemed to fit together like puzzle pieces. Only they know how many arguments they overcame to get to a place of committed life together. And only they know the daily sacrifices and daily joys of the most mundane activities that constitute a relationship. Together, Connie and Karen alone concluded that they would make a promise, a vow to one another for the rest of their natural lives. Without our help or sanction, Karen and Connie made private vows to each other. They promised to love, to cherish, to honor, for better or for worse, for richer or for poorer, in sickness and in health, until they are parted by death.

And yet we have weddings and are gathered here today to make these private vows into public vows. Marriage is about commitment, and it is about covenant. Connie and Karen, you made a covenant before God. You promised and promise to include God in your relationship. You promised

---

1. McFague, *Metaphorical Theology*, 98.

## Part One: Calling for Equality

and promise to treat each other with reverence and respect worthy of all of God's creation. You asked and ask God's blessing on every joyful moment, every difficult decision, and every heartfelt occasion. You pledged and you continue to pledge to each other, and to God, to give this relationship your very best. You are saying that you don't attempt this without God.

And we stand here today to covenant with your commitment. As your community, family, and friends, we are witnesses covenanting to you in your commitment. We promise to listen, to encourage, and to support. We promise to sustain, to care for, to advise, and to counsel. We promise to enrich your lives as much as we know how. As your community, we covenant to surround you with our love as you grow in your love for each other.

In this sense, private love becomes a public affair. And there are the opposites again. What is private has become public. What is personal—as the feminist slogan goes—is political. What is intimate is actually communal.

You have told us that this—like all weddings—is a celebration and blessing. The couple celebrates their love and their relationship; the community blesses them into their future.

Karen and Connie celebrate the love they share and have shared for the past fifteen years and ask for our blessings and support as they move into the future. It is a celebration of the love you already have and a blessing for your days ahead. With rings and promises and your daily lives, you celebrate your love for one another. And us? We bless you with our presence and support and gifts.

Your wedding and your lives are a parable to us. And this is how Jesus tells us about the community of God. In parables. So much so that many theologians have argued that the parables are the most authentic of Jesus' words, and that lifting up—that is, envisioning and teaching about—this ideal community of God was one of the primary purposes of Jesus' ministry.

So here it is again: the community of God is like a college-educated woman who declares that she would give up her well-paying job with benefits, work by day at the gas station down the street to pay her bills, and work by night at the Quick Mart up the road for money to buy gifts if this is what she has to do to be closer to her beloved.

This is what a parable is like. This is what the community of God is like. In the community of God, "events occur and decisions are made which are absurd, radical, alien, extreme." And this is what God wants of us—an extreme quality in our passion for God and for love and for the world.[2]

2 Ibid., 46.

To be so passionate about God and love and the world that its importance overrides everything else in our lives.

After all, that last story—that is what Karen said about Connie one night at dinner just a couple of months ago. "I would give up my job and work by day at the gas station down the street to pay my bills and then by night at the Quick Mart to buy Connie gifts if that is what I had to do to be close to Connie." Connie and Karen have found their pearl of great price in each other. And in this love for each other and God and the world, they have led countercultural lives. They have forsaken not just "all others," as the traditional vows go, but all the privileges of socially affirmed heterosexual love. At times that has meant their personal comfort, their safety, their families, their churches, and their equal rights. And they do this, I dare to say, not just because they love each other, but in order to show us a glimpse of the community of God.

And they *can* do this because of their faith. Because, as McFague notes, "religious people are less comfortable in the world [precisely because they are] aware of the difference between things as they are and things as they ought to be."[3] Loving boldly and unapologetically and with open arms is how Karen and Connie live out their faith in the world. It should be the standard for all of us.

The question before us all today is this: What is your pearl of great price? This is not just a question about who you love or what God you believe in. It's a question about your foolhardy heart. It's a question about your extreme passion. For whom or what would you lose your mind and good sense—or actually find it? What is your pearl of great price? Who or what do you value as much as life itself? What is your pearl of great price? Who or what motivates you to do things in ways completely the opposite of the conventional wisdom around you? What is your pearl of great price? What decisions do you make with full knowledge that you may be uncomfortable, unsafe, and unaccompanied? What is your pearl of great price? Where have you experienced unearned acceptance and unmerited love? That is, where have you experienced the community of God in this world, and what do you do to sustain it?

Jesus says: The community of God is like a woman in search of fine pearls who, on finding one pearl of great price, went and sold all of her possessions and bought it.

---

3 Ibid., 65.

# 3

# The Biblical Support for Same-Sex Marriage

RITA NAKASHIMA BROCK

In addition to being a Commissioned Minister in the Christian Church (Disciples of Christ), the Reverend Dr. Rita Nakashima Brock is currently Research Professor in Theology and Culture and Director of the Soul Repair Center at Brite Divinity School. She is an award-winning author whose books include, most recently, *Soul Repair: Recovery from Moral Injury after War* and *Saving Paradise: How Christianity Traded Love of This World for Crucifixion and Empire*. She is also the first Asian American woman to earn a doctorate in theology. A version of this sermon originally appeared as a blog post in the Religion section of the *Huffington Post* and was adapted for this book.

---

*Genesis 2:18*

In August 2010, Judge Vaughn Walker issued a decision against enforcement of California's Proposition 8 prohibiting same-sex marriage. In light of election results in 2012, his ruling is prescient, and it should please anyone who believes in justice and equality under the law. Though conservative Christians claimed his ruling threatened "Bible-believing Christians," I beg to differ.

I've read the Bible pretty carefully (I read it cover to cover when I was in high school) and even taught it as a college professor. It is not a source I'd turn to in order to defend "traditional" marriage—in its modern definition of one man and one woman. However, the Bible does offer ways to think about *ethical* marriage.

The Bible presents multiple views of marriage, and most actual marriages it depicts are terrible by modern standards. "Traditional" marriages in ancient biblical times, often polygamous, were arranged as transfers of the ownership of daughters. The tenth commandment lists wives among properties like houses and slaves: "You shall not covet your neighbor's house; you shall not covet your neighbor's wife, or male or female slave, or ox, or donkey, or anything that belongs to your neighbor" (Exod 20:17).

Biblical marriages occurred via deception, kidnapping, adulterous seductions, theft, rape, and murder. Wives were often in multiples so that the *paterfamilias* could amass land, flocks, and progeny and cement political alliances. Abraham, David, and Solomon had marriages that would be illegal today. The book of Hosea likens the mercy of God to a husband who has the right to beat or kill his adulterous wife but spares her—for a husband like this, she was supposed to be grateful. When women sought marriages, such as the kind Naomi arranged for Ruth, it was to avoid an even worse fate such as destitution.

The ideal of a housewife found in Proverbs 31 suggests that a decent married life for some women might have been possible in biblical times, but actual examples are rare. It's a telling fact that at Christian weddings today, passages of Scripture used in the service mostly *avoid* marriage texts in the Bible. Instead, ministers tend to use passages that

- *extol love between two women*: "Your people shall be my people" (Ruth 1:16);
- *lift up communitarian values*: "The greatest of these is love" (1 Cor 13:13); or
- *describe erotic passion between unmarried lovers*: "Set me as a seal upon your heart" (Song 8:6—some people are shocked to find the Song of Songs in the Bible at all!).

In the Christian section of the Bible, Jesus and Paul disagreed about what marriage was supposed to be. The difference between them is striking: Jesus thinks of marriage as divinely sanctified; Paul thinks of it as an option

## Part One: Calling for Equality

for the morally weak who need to avoid fornicating. They lived around the same time, and both were Jews, so it's a bit puzzling why they differ so radically, perhaps as puzzling as why, today, some Christians vehemently oppose marriage equality while others support it. Even evangelicals differ: a survey conducted in 2008 found that 26 percent of adults under age thirty supported marriage equality, while only 9 percent of their elders did.[1]

So let's at least get clear about one important fact: there is no "Christian view" of marriage; there are different Christian views, even if you follow the Bible, depending on whether you go with Jesus or with Paul. For over a millennium, the Christian church in Europe leaned toward the latter. It did not sanctify marriage but regarded it as a civil ceremony instead.

Paul, a citizen of the Roman Empire, spent time in jail for opposing that empire, and his negative view of marriage was likely another form of resistance. Other celibate religious movements of his time also saw avoidance of marriage and procreation as a form of resistance to the empire and a sign of a new kind of religious society.

Why was marriage such a huge political issue during Paul's time? During the two decades before Jesus was born, the Roman Empire passed a slew of regulations called the Julian marriage laws. They forced marriage on all Roman citizens. To have enough tax revenues and soldiers for its military legions, the empire needed an expanding citizen population, but the population was shrinking. The situation was dire because average life expectancy was only twenty-five years, and two-thirds of all infants died. Just to stay even, the state required a five-child birthrate per woman. Many elite Roman families resented military conscription of their sons and found the tax burdens excessive. Hence, refusing to marry was a way to resist imperial exploitation.

In addition to such political pressures, Paul may also have rejected marriage because it separated sex and love. Under Roman marriage laws and customs, sex was a function of male domination and aggression. Princeton historian Peter Brown, in his study of this period, *The Body and Society*, wryly remarks that the Romans viewed male adolescents as "human espresso machines";[2] they were always near a sexual boil, ready to erupt. In *Love Between Women*, her careful study of documents from this period, Bernadette Brooten notes that a *paterfamilias* could have sex

---

1. *Religion & Ethics NewsWeekly*, "Young Evangelical Christians and the 2008 Election."
2. Brown, *Body and Society*, 17.

with anyone under his authority and economic control, which meant virtually any female, as well as boys and male slaves. The only people a head of household could *not* have sex with were his equals or superiors, including female superiors, like goddesses or his mother. E. J. Graff, in her book *What Is Marriage For?*, notes that rape of the bride was commonly expected, and in wedding ceremonies, the groom and father-in-law exchanged the vows, since women were exchanged as property and could not take vows. While marriages might have love in them, this was not expected.

For married women, sex was for procreation—a dangerous destiny at a time without reliable birth control or adequate maternal medical care. That women had sexual desires and enjoyed sex was not doubted, but respectable women confined these to the marriage bed. Brooten found that while male homosexual orientations were regarded as immutably determined by astrological influences, lesbianism was regarded as a medical disorder because sex must have domination and subordination. Women's sexual relationships lacked a dominant inserter and subordinate receiver and were, thus, an unnatural disorder.

The construction of sex as male dominance and female subordination may be why Christian conservatives obsess over rare biblical texts against homosexual practices, while they tend to forgive male heterosexual adultery as a lesser sin, even though adultery is clearly condemned in the Ten Commandments but homosexuality is not. It is also true that many of the powerful biblical patriarchs were adulterers. Of course, a sin much more frequently condemned in the Bible is usury, but I digress . . .

Paul believed love was the highest value—even suggesting that in Christ there is *no distinction* between male and female! Whereas sex was a huge problem. He advocated abstinence, though this suggestion has led some to regard him as psychologically disturbed. But, perhaps he was morally disturbed by the Roman marriage system. Ironically, current condemnations of Paul's version of ascetic Christianity exist side by side with great admiration for monastic figures such as the Dalai Lama or the pope. But religious abstinence is also another discussion.

Here is an important distinction between Paul and Jesus: Jesus' view of marriage in Matthew 19 was not based on the Roman version. Unlike Paul, Jesus, a Jewish peasant, was not a Roman citizen. So his view of marriage is grounded in Genesis 2. Conservatives like to use Genesis 2 to defend marriage as between one man and one woman for procreative purposes only (i.e., as authorizing sex between one dominant inserter and one subordinate receiver). However, I don't think this is what Jesus meant in using this text.

A careful look at Genesis, provided by scholar Phyllis Trible, offers an interesting interpretation. She notes that God creates an earthling, *adam*, and breathes divine Spirit into him to make him come alive. All the animals are insufficient to satisfy the *adam*'s needs for a helper. *Ezer kenegdo*, translated "help meet," literally means an equal helper. "Helper," *ezer*, by itself, referred to a superior, such as God. Hence, the addition of *kenegdo* ("corresponding to it") modified *ezer* to suggest an equal. God divides *adam* into *ish*, male, and *isha*, female. Made of the same flesh, Eve is neither superior nor subordinate to Adam. Given that the woman's subordination to the man and painful childbirth were a punishment inflicted in Genesis 3, I think the text of Genesis 2 challenges "traditional marriage" with its male dominance as not being divinely ordained. Inside paradise, God intended relationships of companionship based on equality.[3]

Jesus had to go all the way back to the paradise garden to find a model of what he thought marriage ought to be. Given that model, he accepts divorce. He observed that Moses created divorce because men behaved badly (he calls them hard-hearted, which means unloving). His use of Genesis 2 is a condemnation of the traditional biblical marriage of female subordination inflicted in Genesis 3. He also conceded that the demands of marriage were not for everyone, and remaining unmarried was also okay.

Arguments for California's Prop. 8, which Judge Walker overturned, narrowed the purpose of marriage to procreation. However, neither Paul nor Jesus explicitly mentioned procreation as a reason for marriage. While I don't think Jesus was talking about same-sex marriages, his reference to Genesis 2 grounded marriage in equality and companionship.

While Jesus and Paul differ on marriage, they differ for the same reason. They uphold love as the highest divine good, not women's sexual subordination. In fact, because of the nasty history of institutional marriage in the Bible and heterosexist civil laws that are built on male dominance and female subordination, I think marriage equality means such gender inequality should *not* be inscribed as a necessary basis of marriage.

In his carefully written decision, Judge Walker remarked on changes that have eliminated most of the values and reasons for traditional marriage. He noted that marriage had recently been transformed "from a

3. See Trible, *God and the Rhetoric of Sexuality*, 90.

male-dominated institution into an institution recognizing men and women as equals."[4] The changes also reflect cultural ideas that marriage is a union of love that includes sexual relationship, but not necessarily procreation. They do not nullify marriage per se:

> The evidence shows that the movement of marriage away from a gendered institution and toward an institution free from state-mandated gender roles reflects an evolution in the understanding of gender rather than a change in marriage. The evidence did not show any historical purpose for excluding same-sex couples from marriage, as states have never required spouses to have an ability or willingness to procreate in order to marry. Rather, the exclusion exists as an artifact of a time when the genders were seen as having distinct roles in society and in marriage. That time has passed.[5]

Judge Walker ruled that the state's interest in marriage is guided by the rights of equal protection, not by religion, and that religious ideas should not determine marriage law. His reasoning suggests that legal same-sex weddings are a right that cannot be decided by majority vote.

A number of Christian groups in California, as well as Reformed Jews and Unitarian Universalists, would agree. Proposition 8 denied the constitutional free practice of religion by prohibiting some religious leaders from authorizing same-sex marriages even though their traditions support it. Even worse, Prop. 8 denied the basic human right of marriage to a group of people based on unfounded biases about their sexual orientation. Same-sex couples, like heterosexual couples, offer each other love, companionship, and a stable family environment for raising children.

If marriage is good for society, and equality is the ethical basis for marriage, then gender difference is irrelevant. Marriage equality is good for everyone, including Bible-believing Christians.

---

4. Walker, "Perry v. Schwarzenegger," 112.
5 Ibid., 113.

# 4

## Descriptive or Definitive?

### DAVID J. LOSE

The Reverend Dr. David J. Lose is an ordained minister in the Evangelical Lutheran Church in America who was recently named President of the Lutheran Theological Seminary at Philadelphia. Previously, he served as the Marbury E. Anderson Professor of Biblical Preaching at Luther Seminary in St. Paul, Minnesota, and as the Director of the Center for Biblical Preaching at Luther Seminary, where he created www.WorkingPreacher.org. He has written books for popular audiences such as *Making Sense of Scripture* as well as books for pastors such as *Confessing Jesus Christ: Preaching in a Postmodern World*, which was named one of the "Top 10 Books of 2004" by the Academy of Parish Clergy. His most recent book is *Preaching at the Crossroads: How the World—and Our Preaching—Is Changing*. You can find his writing on preaching and other matters of faith and life at his blog, ". . .in the Meantime" (davidlose.net).

---

*Romans 6:3–4; 8:14–17*

My life, like yours, is filled with a lot of what I would call "happens-to-be" truths. Do you know what I mean? Let me offer a few examples.

I happen to live in St. Paul, Minnesota.

## Descriptive or Definitive? · Lose

I happen to teach at Luther Seminary.

I happen to be married.

I happen to have two children.

I happen to be forty-eight years old.

I happen to love pizza.

I happen to be six feet tall, slightly overweight, and in only fair shape. (And yes, those last two were hard to admit.)

I happen to be the fourth of five children.

I happen to love playing tennis and board games, especially with my kids.

And I happen to be curiously moved each fall by the fate of grown men dressed in purple and gold playing their hearts out on the green fields of athletic competition.

Do you see what I mean? All of these facts about me are true, but they are "happen-to-be" truths.

I mean, I have lived other places than St. Paul and likely will again.

I didn't always teach at Luther and at some point no longer will.

There was a time when I was single and, although it's painful to contemplate, know that I could be at some point again.

I once had no children and thought for a long time I would have more.

I wasn't always forty-eight years old and in just a few months won't be ever again.

Depending on where I grew up, perhaps I would have grown to love raw fish rather than pizza.

I spent most of my early years well below six feet and, if we're going to be perfectly honest, am no longer quite that tall as the pull of gravity and age have started to take their toll. And I am committed to not being overweight in the future and getting back into shape.

I have four siblings, but my parents will be the first to tell you that was not by design.

It could be that, had I moved to Minnesota earlier, I'd play hockey instead of tennis and want to ice-fish with my kids instead of playing games.

And although I bleed purple in support of the Vikings each fall during football season, it wasn't always this way, and perhaps someday I'll root for the colors of another team, maybe—*although this feels like a stretch*—even the green and gold of the Packers.

And that's what I mean, you see. That my life—and yours too—is filled with these "happen-to-be" truths that while very important to us, ultimately only *describe* us, not *define* us. That is, precisely because all the things I mentioned could have been otherwise, none of them defines who I am. They are descriptively true—and important—but not definitive.

In these passages from his Letter to the Romans, the Apostle Paul invites us to imagine the one thing about us that *is* truly definitive. Paul reminds his readers—then and now—that when we were baptized into Christ, we were baptized into his death and raised with him into new life. And in this dying and rising we were joined to Christ, named as God's own children, and granted life in and through the Holy Spirit.

This, Paul claims, is the *one* thing that defines us: we are God's children. It could be no other way. It is the one thing that when everything else is taken away from us will be the only thing that remains. Even should the day come when many of those descriptively true things about me have changed, or should I over time or because of age begin to forget them, yet I will still be God's child. This will not change, cannot change. That is God's promise, the promise uttered by the one who created the world out of nothing and raises the dead to life.

Oh, by the way: there's one other "happens-to-be" truth about myself I failed to mention. I happen to be heterosexual. I *happen* to be. I could have been otherwise. I know plenty of people who are. But I happen to be heterosexual—this is both descriptively true about me and important, as it has shaped much of my adult life. And I know that is the case with many persons I know, both heterosexual and homosexual—our sexual orientation is descriptively true and important.

But in the recent discussions and debates over human sexuality, I think we have come dangerously close to speaking and acting as if our sexual orientation is not merely descriptive, but actually definitive. And in doing so we risk the primacy of our baptismal identity, as if somehow what's most important to us is *not* that we are God's children, not that Christ died for us, not that Christ was raised for our justification, but rather that whether we are attracted to persons of the opposite or same sex is the be-all and end-all of our existence.

Is our sexual orientation descriptively true? Yes. Is it important? Absolutely. Does it define us? No! Or, to borrow the words of the Apostle Paul in the verses just before those we started with, "Hell no!"[1] (Which is a more accurate description of the Greek phrase *me genoito* that Paul uses to answer in the absolute negative some of the rhetorical questions he asks.)

---

1. Rom 6:2.

So if there is one thing I would like to add to the ongoing debates about human sexuality that have consumed so much of our time and energy in recent years, it is to advocate that we do not look to find our common, shared, and definitive identity in our sexuality any more than we would in our present residence, height and weight, or favorite sports team.

I realize that does not settle all the questions about same-sex marriage. I realize that people hold different points of view and that they will continue to do so. And I realize that these differences are important. But they are not ultimate.

Christians throughout the centuries, in fact, have disagreed on many important matters. But at their best they have also tried to make an important distinction between primary and secondary concerns—between, that is, those things that hold ultimate significance and those that, while important, do not. And according to the Apostle Paul, what is of primary significance is our baptismal identity not simply as children of God but also, as Paul writes, "as heirs of God and joint heirs with Christ" (Rom 8:17).

*Joint heirs!* Can you believe that? That God regards us as worthy of the same inheritance as Christ? On what grounds? Surely not by our own merit or accomplishment. Rather, God names us as children and counts us as coheirs with Christ by grace alone.

For there is another thing that has defined us. We all, as Paul writes earlier in this same letter, "have sinned and fall short of the glory of God" and therefore are all "now justified by his grace as a gift" (Rom 3:23–24).

This also does not settle all the questions before us, but perhaps it can offer some guidance. For the law, from this point of view, does not solve the problem of broken, sinful humanity. Rather, it offers us a modicum of relief and help by providing counsel and setting boundaries as we make our way through this difficult life. From this point of view, institutions like marriage help us lead more productive and perhaps even happier lives, but they do not redeem sinful lives. So while my heterosexual marriage offers a measure of fulfillment by setting boundaries, encouraging fidelity, and in this way providing a measure of stability, it unfortunately does not prevent me from sinning. (Just ask my wife!) And, indeed, I have found forgiveness as the only rival to love as the most important part of a successful relationship. So my marriage, while it helps me live more fully in this world, does not make me holy, righteous, or perfect. That is by God's grace alone.

For this reason, I think same-sex marriage may offer a measure of stability by setting boundaries and encouraging fidelity. It will not stop sin

PART ONE: CALLING FOR EQUALITY

or convey righteousness; that is by God's grace alone. But it will help any number of God's children live more fully into the abundant life here and now that God desires for all God's children, homosexual and heterosexual alike.

Of course, even in naming ourselves this way—that is, by dividing us into categories based on our sexual orientation—I run the risk of making it sound like sexual orientation is the most important characteristic about us and thereby fail to honor the God-given gift of identity and life Paul proclaims in this passage.

So let me try it this way, borrowing again the language of the apostle: we are those forgiven sinners whom God declares also to be children of God, and not only children but also heirs of God and joint heirs with Christ. And to God's beloved children—*all* God's beloved children—God gives two gifts. First, God gives the gift of the law, which includes marriage, to guide us in our lives, set boundaries that permit us to flourish, and help us discover a modicum of stability and joy in this challenging world. And second, God gives us the gift of the gospel, which reminds us that even the law and our attempts to discern and keep it do not define us, for we are defined by God's gracious gift of the Spirit that invites each and all of us to call out in wonder and joy, "Abba, Father" (Rom 8:15).

Thanks be to God. Amen.

# 5

## Looking for Love

### W. Scott Haldeman

As the Associate Professor of Worship at Chicago Theological Seminary (CTS), Dr. Scott Haldeman has served as faculty advisor to the Heyward Boswell Society, an organization of LGBTQ and queer-affirming students at CTS, since 2009. His first book, *Towards Liturgies of Reconciliation*, analyzes the role of racism in the development of U.S. Protestant worship. In queer religious studies, examples of his recent work include "A Queer Fidelity," which was published in the journal *Theology and Sexuality*, and "Receptivity and Revelation," which appears in the book *Body and Soul: Rethinking Sexuality as Justice-Love*. Dr. Haldeman identifies himself as "a baptized Christian of Presbyterian persuasion." This sermon was preached at Glenview Community Church in Glenview, Illinois, on July 3, 2011.

---

*Genesis 24:34–38, 42–49, 58–67 · Song of Songs 2:8–13*

We gather today at the intersection of several calendars: the lectionary, the national civil religion calendar, and the legislative calendar which recently includes the disruption of business as usual with the legalization of civil unions for same-sex (and different-sex) couples in Illinois at the start of June and the passage of a marriage rights bill in New York State at month's end, making New York the sixth state along with the District of Columbia to allow same-sex couples full access to the protections, benefits, and responsibilities of marriage—at the state level, at least. To me, this coincidence of dates on a lovely sunny day when one might put on a pair of swimming trunks and a T-shirt and head to the lake brings to mind memories of those sweet summer loves—and so today I intend to speak of matters of the heart and how we are all, in different ways of course, "looking for love . . ."

The lectionary tells us it is ordinary time, the annual summer season when our Scripture selections are not governed by the great feasts of Easter and Christmas—and so the great themes of the paschal mystery and the incarnation—but instead by a certain leisure to explore various books not usually highlighted "in course"—which means that we are encouraged to work our way through them chapter by chapter. One book highlighted now is Genesis and its stories of the patriarchs and matriarchs—Abraham and Sarah, Isaac and Rebekah, and Jacob and his many wives and twelve sons, the forebears of the twelve tribes.

Today's story is a love story. Romantic, is it not? "[And Isaac] . . . took Rebekah, and she became his wife, and he loved her" (Gen 24:67). And the screen fades to black as the young lovers kiss . . . Ah, yes, another Hollywood tale ends with the girl getting the guy and living happily ever after.

Rebekah might be the speaker in the text from the Song of Solomon: "Look, [Isaac] comes, leaping upon the mountains, bounding over the hills. My beloved is like a gazelle, or a young stag" (Song 2:8–9).

And Isaac says in return, "Arise, [Rebekah,] my love, my fair one, and come away; for now the winter is past, the rain is over and gone. The flowers appear on the earth; the time of singing has come" (Song 2:10–12).

But such joyful, passionate attachment only appears at the very end of our tale, and as the final paragraph continues we find what is probably not the sort of ending for which most of us would be looking in a tale of romance: "So Isaac was comforted after his mother's death" (Gen 24:67). That's not the unbridled, free-flowing, rather graphic passion of the Song, is it? It points instead to the daily grind of a woman meeting the needs and wants of a man overly attached to his now dead mother—we do know that kind of story, do we not?

So perhaps the romance we want to see is not really there. Let's look more closely, shall we? At the time of the scene that opens our story, it is time for Isaac to be married. Abraham wants his wife to be "our kind of people." He sends an unnamed servant back to the land that he had left at God's command, back to the land where his own relatives remained behind. The servant has not a clue who these people are. He puts the onus on God, saying, "Let the one who comes to the well and who agrees to give me a drink and also to draw water for my camels be the one who will be Isaac's wife."[1]

And just then, apparently, Rebekah arrives, carrying her jar. She responds to the servant exactly as he predicted. She must be the one. The servant talks to her brother. Laban asks Rebekah if she is willing to leave all she knows and all those whom she currently loves to go get hitched to a stranger's son—a reportedly wealthy stranger but a stranger nonetheless. She gets on her camel and rides. She sees Isaac; he sees her; they wed—and along the way, they begin to fall in love.

Now, I'll wager, fairy safely, I think, that there are very few among those gathered in Glenview, Illinois, in July 2011, who experienced an arranged marriage. Further, I doubt we would want to arrange the marriages of our daughters and sons. But, thinking broadly about human history, such was the common practice until relatively recently—and still today, in some cultures, it is not unknown.

The point is that marriage is not static but has changed—and continues to. Opponents of allowing gay men and lesbian women access to marriage tend to ignore the shifts—fairly major ones in this central human institution. Of course, proponents often do the same, struggling for access to this supposedly crucial and unchanging social institution for some who fit quite easily into its traditions—except for one (might not one say) relatively minor detail—rather than reimagining alternatives that honor the variety of human intimate relations for all. Perhaps a quick review of the major models would be a helpful reminder to us—and would better inform our debates in ways that may both clarify and complicate the opposing arguments.

I'm thinking of four models of marriage at the moment and seek only to highlight the shifts in each period as examples of how marriage has in fact changed.

First, in the pre-Christian era, marriage was fundamentally and basically a simple exchange of property—a woman and her dowry were given to a man, who then had allegiance to the woman's father—for the purposes of creating clear lines of lineage, inheritance, and alliance. Prior to any notion of individual agency for the couple, fathers (perhaps with a bit of counsel from mothers, but often not) entered into marriage contracts with other

---

1. See Gen 24:14.

fathers. In a positive sense, such marriages functioned as a way to negotiate peaceably the relations not just between the two central characters but larger family units, tribes, even nations. We don't want to return here but the reminder that more is at stake in the relationship than the happiness of two love-struck lunatics may be helpful. And, of course, like Isaac and Rebekah, sometimes love blooms in any case.

The early church made significant changes. Most importantly, marriage was subordinated to other aspects of discipleship. While marriage was spoken of as a gift from God for companionship and the begetting of children, it was also the second best choice for followers of the Crucified One. It was better to remain unencumbered by such obligations and attachments in order to be free to spread the good news and face persecution. Marriage came to be thought of as a compromise for those who were unable to abstain from sex altogether—as Paul put it, and I paraphrase, "It is better to marry than to burn (but even better, perhaps, not to have heat at all)."[2] For those who did choose to marry, the church also borrowed heavily from the surrounding culture—yes, the ring and the dress (though not a white gown yet—that had to wait for Queen Victoria), but more importantly, we took from the Romans their emphasis on consent—that both parties had to be free from coercion as they came before the community to declare their solemn vows. The suspicion that any sex, even of the vanilla type in a marriage bed, could be free of desire (and so must be sinful) resulted not only in a celibate priesthood in most of the Western church but also in teachings and even laws that regulated the acts of intimacy between married couples and denied any legitimate sexual activity to everyone else. This remains a mess that we continue to sort out today, but we cannot attempt a resolution to such problems here. Just a final note that liturgically marriage and the wedding were not fully integrated into the Western sacramental system until the twelfth century—when, among others, Peter Lombard codified the sacraments as seven in number, and marriage as one of the seven, in his classic book *The Sentences*. Twelve hundred years . . . hmmm!

But we must jump another three hundred years or so and glance at the central Protestant schools of thought. Luther thought everyone should marry, including clergy, overturning the hierarchy of values in which celibacy was the ideal. At the same time, he also downgraded marriage—from a sacrament to a social contract since, in his view, in itself marriage contains no promise of God's grace for us—and don't we all know something about

2. See 1 Cor 7:9.

that lack! Marriage then functioned as a recognized relationship of mutual care of husband and wife and a channel for legitimate sexual expression and a container in which the next generation of children could be raised in the faith. But it was an arrangement of this world, the earthly kingdom—not of the divine reign that was surely coming and where no such disciplinary structures would be required. Calvin followed Luther in most respects but gave less authority to the civil government in defining and regulating marriage. Marriage was for him an establishment of covenantal relations of accountability of the couple to each other, with God, with the wider families, with the church, and with the civil state. The Anglicans tweaked marriage a bit further, employing the metaphor of "commonwealth" and so emphasizing marriage as a building block in which the rule of a husband over wife, children, and property reflects on a smaller scale the relations of the magistrate to town and king or queen to nation. The household was a little kingdom—the kingdom, the empire, a big household. These glimpses at the positions of the reformers clearly indicate areas of both continuity and discontinuity with the pre-Reformation understandings. Suspicion about whether any sex can be good remains—along with the exception that marriage provides some measure of justification since procreation has its imperatives. At the same time, marriage is both elevated as most appropriate for most people rather than a concession to weakness and downgraded from sacrament to an earthly estate alongside church and state as an arena of rules and regulations and oversight to protect the weak and foster the growth and health of a society.

Our final stop today is the Enlightenment, in which marriage becomes primarily a contract between two persons like any other transaction. It can then be shaped according to the desires of the parties as they wish, and it can be broken when obligations go unfulfilled. The state, which expanded its reach into marriage forcefully and in a variety of different ways in the Reformation period, at this point asserts almost full authority. As we know even today, wedding ceremonies may happen in churches as well as in courthouses, but, even in sacred spaces, clergy function as civil agents as they sign a license issued by the state—not the other way around.

There is much more to say about how marriage has changed—for further details, I recommend the book *From Sacrament to Contract*, by Professor John Witte Jr. of Princeton University, from which my brief notes were drawn—but it is the fact of change that is crucial.

And, lest this sermon morph into a history lecture, let me shift again back to our national calendar. It is Fourth of July weekend, of course—a time to celebrate the birth of our nation as independent from British authority. Those who signed the Declaration of Independence not only started a war but also began to think anew about the other relationships that structure human lives. A major contribution to thought about marriage arose then too. Beholden to the British king and so immersed in the Anglican "commonwealth" model of marriage, among others, as mentioned above, some of the American revolutionaries made the connection between the various household metaphors. If the colonies were compelled by unjust treatment to break with England, should not also one who suffers unjustly at the hands of one's more local sovereign—for example, one's husband—have the right to break the contract as well? They answered yes, but the complete dissolution of what is called "coverture"—the legal doctrine in which a woman renounces any claim to an independent identity as citizen as well as any claim of ownership of her own property when she marries—took another one hundred and fifty years or so to be completed. Still, it was relegated to the dustbin of history—as have been so many other uses of marriage and marriage law to regulate and subordinate minority groups.

Think of Native tribes whose alternative marital relationships were used first as an excuse to obliterate them and later as a reason to remove the children and bring them up as proper little European-American citizens who would enter into Western-style marriages. No more.

Think of miscegenation laws—how marriage and its protections were denied to slaves to protect the prerogatives of the owners but, after the Emancipation Proclamation, marriage was imposed to regulate African American sexuality—while interracial marriage was outlawed in parts of this country until 1957. No longer.

The question to us for today and for tomorrow is this: while we enjoy beer and bratwurst while watching bombs burst in air, what sort of ideals will we celebrate? Will we proclaim simplistically that the U.S. is "number one" despite our continuing failure to treat all citizens equally and to relate justly and peaceably to other nations and peoples, or will we commit to helping this great and troubled land to be, more and more, the land of the free and the home of the brave, a land of equality and justice, a land of opportunity and mutual care, that all might live with a measure of the abundance that we continue to produce but seem to have so much trouble sharing?

Isaac and Rebekah got lucky. A marriage arranged from afar by his father and her brother turned out well—at least for him and his comfort. But theirs is not a model of marriage we aspire to follow. What then shall we do as neighbors and friends ask us to consider if further shifts in the structure and understanding of marriage are allowed? A simple "no" seems too easy, as marriage has changed and is quite likely to continue to change despite protests, no matter how sincere. It is probably wiser, then, to think more deeply about marriage, its historical shifts and its entanglements of theology and law and rights and rites—and, then, to talk to each other about the sorts of privileges and obligations that should accompany various relationships of intimacy, and why. In addition, this holiday reminds us that we must have such conversations with certain assumptions of our nation's birth in view: first, that every human being has inalienable rights, which include the right to life, liberty and the pursuit of happiness; second, that every citizen has the right to be treated equally before the law; and third, that no particular religious view can be imposed on all without straining the credulity of disestablishment beyond recognition.

Further, same-sex couples who want marriage licenses aren't attacking marriage—they are trying to preserve it. Straight folks have mucked marriage up plenty on their own already, right? So can we try a different conversation? Can we consider uncoupling marriage from the myriad social benefits—access to employer insurance coverage (which should also probably be uncoupled), social security survivor benefits, hospital visitation, and so on—in ways that protect the vulnerable without legitimizing some households and delegitimizing others? Just a thought.

In the meantime, we can be assured that the human heart will continue to look for love as we follow one whose very name is love, one who leads us as a pilgrim people on a journey to new lands where nothing will be the same, not even marriage—a time and place where all are welcomed to the feast, where every tear is wiped away, where death's sting is felt no longer, and where all shall be well and all manner of things shall be well.

# 6

## Deeper than Biology

BARBARA K. LUNDBLAD

The Reverend Dr. Barbara K. Lundblad is the distinguished Joe R. Engle Professor of Preaching Emerita at Union Theological Seminary in the City of New York. An ordained minister in the Evangelical Lutheran Church in America, she has taught preaching at Yale Divinity School, Princeton Theological Seminary, Hebrew Union College, and in the DMin program of the Association of Chicago Theological Schools. In 2007, she served as president of the Academy of Homiletics. Her numerous writings related to preaching include *Transforming the Stone* and *Marking Time*. This sermon was preached at the Festival of Homiletics on May 19, 2010.

---

*Genesis 2:18–25*

If I had written the Bible, I would have cleaned it up. One birth story of Jesus rather than one told by Luke and a completely different one told by Matthew—no more confusion about whether to have wise men in the crèche at Christmas or wait until Epiphany! One resurrection account would be enough—the other three would have to go. It's too confusing to have all those different women at the empty tomb. Of course, I'd have to start at the very beginning, for it's quite clear that there are two creation stories. Try hard as we will, we'll never harmonize the two—either male and female were created at the same moment (Gen 1) or man was created first, woman second (Gen 2).

Thankfully, I did not write the Bible. What a wondrous thing it is that different—even contradictory—stories are allowed to stand, often side by side. Though some lament texts that were left out of the biblical canon, it is truly astonishing that very different voices were left in—and it's true from the very beginning. The Bible begins with a Call to Worship—doxology rather than biology. You can hear the litany, each stanza ending with the same pattern: "And there was evening and there was morning, the first day . . . And there was evening and there was morning, the second day." And on to the sixth day: "Then God said, 'Let us make humankind in our image, according to our likeness . . .'"[1]

Even at the beginning, God wasn't alone. Martin Buber heard those plural pronouns and declared, "In the beginning was relation"—God who longed not only to be, but to be-with. "So God created humankind in [God's] image, in the image of God he created them, male and female he created them" (Gen 1:27). The image of God is female and male. All this happens in a moment—both genders created at the same time. "And there was evening and there was morning, the sixth day" (Gen 1:31). And on the seventh day, God rested.

But not for long! In chapter 2, the story starts all over again: "In the day that the LORD God made the earth and the heavens . . ." (Gen 2:4) This is not liturgy. There are no refrains. Scholars are quite sure this second story is older. So shouldn't it be first? In the wisdom of the scribes and the breath of the Spirit, someone knew it was better to begin the Bible with a Call to Worship. Yet, this older story remains. In this story, the man is formed near the beginning, with nothing said about the sun and moon, the seas or dry land: "Then the LORD God formed man [*adam*] from the dust of the ground [*adamah*], and breathed into his nostrils the breath of life; and the man became a living being" (Gen 2:7). God placed the man in a garden—the storyteller even names the rivers that flowed in that garden. It is in this second story that God tells the man he can eat anything in the garden—except fruit from the tree of the knowledge of good and evil.

Then, we come to today's text. God said, "It is not good that the man should be alone; I will make him a helper as his partner" (Gen 2:18). So, God formed the animals and birds! God formed them out of the dust of the

---

1. See Gen 1.

ground, but God did not breathe into them. There was some closer connection between God and the man. God gave the man a big assignment: name all the animals and all the birds of the air. (There's no mention of fish or sea monsters.) How would he know what to call them? This big fellow looks like an elephant to me. And this cuddly creature I will call koala. Tiger. Rhinoceros. Penguin. Hummingbird. Hyena. That animal laughed out loud and so did the man.

But when every animal and bird had been named, God could see that none of them was a fitting partner for the man. So God put the man under anesthesia, took out one of his ribs, and closed up the incision. From that rib God created a woman and brought her to the man. "This at last is bone of my bones and flesh of my flesh" (Gen 2:23), the man said. Later on in Genesis, Laban will say almost these same words when he meets his nephew Jacob for the first time: "Surely you are my bone and my flesh!" (Gen 29:14). You are like me. We are kin. *Adam* had never seen another human being. He was delighted: "Here at last is bone of my bones and flesh of my flesh"—that is, you are not a gerbil or a giraffe! His loneliness was over. God, who longed to be-with, knew *adam* wanted someone to be-with, too.

And from that day on people assumed that a woman had one more rib than a man. Somewhere down the road of history, the study of human skeletons revealed that women and men have the exact same number of ribs. Perhaps the text wasn't written as a treatise on human anatomy. This is not about biology. Yet many people quote these verses in Genesis 2 to prove God's intention for the heterosexual ordering of creation. ("Adam and Eve, not Adam and Steve!") We have asked biological questions of a text that isn't about biology. As the text itself says, this is a story about God's intention for companionship rather than loneliness.

Of course, some of you are waiting for what comes next. For the "therefore..."

"Therefore a man leaves his father and his mother and clings to his wife, and they become one flesh" (Gen 2:24). The language here is a bit different from the earlier verses—as though the moral of an Aesop's fable has been dropped into the story. At this point in Genesis, there was neither father nor mother, nor was there anyone called a "wife." This seems to be a later addition to the story—when there were fathers and mothers and wives. Then, the storyteller returns to tell us the man and woman were naked and unashamed.

I have tried to imagine a wedding shaped by these words—not the naked part, but the first part: "a man leaves his father and mother and clings to his wife." How should we plan a wedding according to this text? The bride and her bridesmaids will be waiting at the front of the church, facing the back. Then, the groomsmen walk up the aisle one by one, turn, and face the congregation. All of them are waiting for the groom. He walks in slowly with his father and mother—I have no idea what the organist will play! I don't know if he's carrying flowers—perhaps a football or an iPad? When the three of them reach the front of the church, the minister asks, "Who gives this man to be married to this woman?" His mother answers, "His father and I do." His parents kiss their son on the cheek and he joins hands with the bride. He leaves his father and mother and clings to his wife. That's what the text describes, doesn't it? Well, we don't need to take the Bible literally on this.

It is this verse in Gen 2 that Jesus quotes in Matthew and in Mark.[2] In both cases, Jesus is speaking a strong word against divorce and remarriage. I wonder if congregations that have left the Episcopal Church for the Anglican Church in America will permit the ordination of people who are divorced and remarried? Will priests in those dioceses allow divorced people to be married in the church? I have the same question about Lutheran churches who have voted to leave the ELCA because we approved the ordination of partnered gay and lesbian people two years ago. It will be sad if they turn divorced people away and refuse the blessing of marriage because people long for companionship. God said it from the beginning: "It is not good for you to be alone. I will make for you a partner."

Genesis 2 is about human relationship more than human anatomy. While the text doesn't affirm gay marriage, it does affirm the goodness of human companionship and the formation of new families. Gay marriage will never damage marriage as much as the infidelity of politicians who have condemned gay marriage. "What makes a relationship moral?" It's not the gender of the partners, but the faithfulness and love the partners have for each other.

When gay and lesbian people come to understand who we are, when we fall in love, we borrow the words of Genesis: "This at last is bone of my bones and flesh of my flesh." Here is a fitting partner for me. What God has joined together let no one—not even the church—rend asunder.

---

2. See Matt 19:5 and Mark 10:7.

*Part Two*

Calling for Liberation

# 7

# Whosoever

### Alton B. Pollard III

The Reverend Dr. Alton B. Pollard III is the Dean and Professor of Religion and Culture at Howard University School of Divinity in Washington, DC. He is an ordained Baptist minister who has held faculty positions at St. Olaf College, Wake Forest University, and Emory University, where he was Director of Black Church Studies at Candler School of Theology and Chair of American Religious Cultures in the Graduate Division of Religion. He is the author of a number of books and articles, including *Mysticism and Social Change*. This sermon was preached as the Banquet Gala Address for the Metropolitan Community Church, People of African Descent National Conference, in Washington, DC, May 22, 2011.

---

*John 3:16*

Hidden in plain sight on the wall behind my desk is a rainbow portrayal of a hauntingly familiar human figure. There is something about the face in the portrait that is darkly radiant and altogether inviting, despite the fact its features are masked by shadows that tell no demographic tale, that reveal not the faintest clue about hair texture or length, fullness of lips or nose, eye color or shape. The figure is adorned in flowing rainbow garments of amber, orange, purple, brown, and green. Set against a multihued backdrop of near three-dimensional quality, however else one may choose to describe it—a stained glass window, iridescent prism, kaleidoscopic canvas, Technicolor optics, shaft of light radiating hope and possibility—the figure in the forefront looms larger than life itself. The person is standing. Waiting. With arms outstretched. With hands held out. With heart open wide. With holes the size of nails visible in each palm. And writ large across the portrait in a rainbow of letters is a single word: "*Whosoever*."[1]

They are among the silent and most silenced members of our community: the despised and rejected ones, the people who have come to know that they have been betrayed, denounced, and abandoned by almost everyone and most especially by the church, their church, the Black church.[2] For these persons, whose stories and struggles have everything to do with matters of human affection, there is the terribly urgent ache to know—to know why it has happened, how it has happened, and why it continues to be this way. The Black church, born out of struggle, which nurtured and empowered a people and affirmed their absolute sense of worth, and whose social legacy is community, solidarity, justice, and freedom, is a church that all too often today is unable to bring itself to accept sexual difference, sexual diversity, sexual identity, sexual equality, sexual affection, sexual love. A church that would rather wallow in its own sexual dysfunction than embrace the entire community of the faithful; a church unable to celebrate the gift of its kith and kin of diverse affection and orientation. A church that is woefully insecure and inarticulate when it comes to matters of human intimacy, that suffers from sexual repression, and that is profoundly ill at ease with the erotic. A church that often overlooks its own misguided sexual politics, peccadillos, and improprieties even as it pronounces judgment on same-gender loving relationships. A church that is suffering, not surprisingly, from a decline in active membership, in relevance, and in influence. Many congregations are in trouble; entire communions are in trouble; the Christian faith is in trouble; our society is in trouble; our souls are in trouble. Today, Black congregations in the United States stand at the crossroads of our liberation once more. How will we respond?

---

1. The original painting *Whosoever* is illustrative of the broadly inclusive church and hangs in the sanctuary of Metropolitan Interdenominational Church in Nashville, Tennessee, where the Reverend Edwin C. Sanders II is Senior Servant. For more on the artwork and congregation, see http://www.micwhosoever.org/.

2. "The Black church" is shorthand for the vast network of racial-ethnic communities of Christian faith, worship, and life born out of and informed by the historic and present-day experiences of people of African descent in the United States.

Our focus in this message is on the most famous and, perhaps, most beloved text in all the biblical record. I well remember reciting John 3:16 in the language of the old King James Version as a child in Sunday school, and some of you still may: "For God so loved the world, that he gave his only begotten Son, that whosoever believeth in him should not perish, but have everlasting life." It is beautifully poetic language that no biblical or cultural exegete worth their salt today would suggest is the most exacting translation. No matter—the passage is so indelibly etched upon our memory, so familiar and so mundane to us, we're sure we already know what it means before we ever read or hear it. John 3:16 turns up at sporting events, at the moment when photojournalists train their lenses on the end zone, home plate, ringside, or courtside for all the world to see. Like *WWJD?* it is instantly recognizable as Christian shorthand for religious faith, a slogan and cliché made popular by people who wear rainbow-colored Afro wigs and carry cardboard signs. For still others, it is a magic formula almost, the missionary's mandated service, the evangelist's code for salvation, a password possessed only by proven believers. And by the time all of us have finished with these words, if we even bother to say the words anymore (for many the reference itself is enough), they have become an empty banality, a sounding brass, a tinkling cymbal. We've heard them before, and so we never really hear them at all.

When I ask myself, as I often do, what it is that I hope to accomplish as a student of religion and life, and as a minister of the gospel, I sometimes think that I would gladly settle for just being able to plumb the depths of meaning found in a single text, yea, even a single word. In that third chapter of the sixteenth verse of the Gospel of John is found one such word for me, a word so subversive, so dangerous, so disturbing it has been disavowed or abandoned by most segments of the church, and all but ignored by biblical scholarship. This word is sidestepped, avoided, buried, and somehow forgotten in a text that is a fervent favorite of traditionalists but finds few postmodern takers. The scholarship on John 3:16 is unclear. Its critics are at cross purposes. It has no exact counterpart in any of the other Gospels. To some, there would seem to be little to commend its canonization. Yet if we have the courage to attend to the heart of this verse we find a word that fires the human imagination and leads into the radical depths. *Whosoever.* Whoever. Everyone. Everybody. "Whosoever," Jesus says, says it to Nicodemus, says it to all of us.

PART TWO: CALLING FOR LIBERATION

In America's churches of African descent we have long said the same thing that Jesus said, only with lyric cultural improvisation we have said it thus: "Whosoever will, let her or him come." Sunday after Sunday it remains the custom, without respect of denomination or creed, for Black congregations across the country to "open the doors of the church" after the sermon, to extend the invitation to meet Jesus, to renew one's commitment to discipleship, to come forward for special prayer needs, to become a part of the community of saints, to receive all the rights and privileges pertaining thereunto—to make this your "church home." It is a centuries-old tradition, dating back to the time of the enslavement of our ancestors in this land, when African and New World sacred views met, and seekers came to the mourner's bench, surrounded by the Elders, the Deacons, the Mothers' Boards, the Prayer Warriors, the Sanctified Saints, in hopes of hearing Jesus call her or his name. Even now, I can hear someone singing, "I told Jesus it will be alright if he changes my name." I can hear someone else testifying, "I got a new name over in Zion, and it's mine, mine, mine."

Yes, from the very beginning, ritual membership in the "household of faith" affirmed every individual's experience as the key that unlocks the door to mystic communion. In the giving and receiving of the right hand of fellowship, Black folk came to understand their God-given right as a people to have, hold, and express a profound sense of themselves in their full and embodied humanity, inclusive of their sexuality. To this very day the great invitation remains unchanged. Jesus says there is no test of eligibility; there are no qualifications for fitness. Every child of God has equal access to this spiritual life; no person lies beyond the pale. The enabling words of the old Negro spiritual have it right: "I've got a right, you've got a right, we've all got a right to the tree of life."

Now what I would like to suggest in connection with the great invitation is that somewhere along the way the Black church lost its way. In the transition "from slavery to freedom" we began to establish social, cultural, and theological tests for inclusion in the body, neglecting the divine criterion of "whosoever" in the process. When I think about the tough, hammered-out, often brutal experiences that we have endured as a people, how "through many dangers, toils, and snares we have already come"; when my soul looks back and wonders "how we got over," I know it was the hand of the Lord, I know it was God who made a way out of no way. Yet when I am brought face to face today with the implications of the great invitation, and when I engage the unjust economic, physical, and sociopolitical realities around me, of this I am equally sure: the work of God's church is far from over—it has only just begun.

As a once disinherited people, we have known something about searing brands and burning flesh, iron chains and fetters and being locked away. We have known what it is to be sold downriver and sold out, about plantations and overseers, slave drivers and patty-rollers, the KKK and Citizens' Councils, untold rapings and lynchings, and Jane and Jim Crow. We are also acquainted with far more recent cruelties, with official policies, customs, and institutions that work to subdue us behind concrete walls and iron bars and glass ceilings and railroad tracks and tracking systems and media lynchings and gentrification and gerrymandering and annexation and the annihilation of our humanity. We know about police crackdowns and crack houses and roadblocks and cell blocks and lockdowns and indecency and detention and "law and order" and profiling and the New Jim Crow assault on our communities.

But we have also come to know far more than we are willing to admit, and more than we care to discuss, about other equally painful realities, powerful prejudices, searing hatreds, legal pogroms, social indignities, moral revulsions, derisive fears directed at persons and groups solely or largely for reasons of sexuality and/or gender. We know about patriarchy and misogyny and emotional and physical humiliation and sexual harassment in the workplace and sexual violence in the home and sexual impropriety from the pulpit to the pew to the public square. We know about hierarchies of power and "special rights" polemics and sexism and heterosexism and homophobia and hate crimes and gay-bashing and lesbian-bashing and opposition to marriage equality and HIV disease, dis-ease and death. We know about the suffering and rejection and alienation and exclusion and subordination and condemnation and devaluation and discrimination of those who live on the margins of the marginalized, who are the very oppressed of the oppressed, who are the sexually battered and abused and sick and dying, who are lesbian and gay and bisexual and transgender and questioning and queer and straight, who are our sisters and brothers and beloved partners and friends, who are we ourselves. We know, we know, we know because we who claim to be the church have betrayed them.

God knows all of this, of course, knows that even at our best humanity, no less the church, only sees through a glass darkly. We, all of us, have had shadows, echoes, dreams, experiences, those odd moments in our lives, glimpses of something dimly seen or dimly heard, a far country, a sense of something deeply hidden within. We hear a voice, unlike any other voice, for it speaks to us audibly and distinctly and without sound—and it is all the more powerful for being without sound—"*whosoever.*" We listen to the *sensus numinous*, the sound of the genuine, the movement of the Spirit, the radical imperative, the divine eruption taking place in our hearts, if only for a whispering moment, and then we start to move without really knowing what to believe either about the voice or about ourselves. And yet we go, for the truth of the matter is we already know what the voice has to say: we have not been willing to risk ourselves without reservation. We have not offered the world very much at all in the way of visionary leadership. We have not been in empathetic relationship, compassionate connection, or moral solidarity, one to another. We have not been willing to transgress our comfort zones of affection, religion, socioeconomic location, or race. We have not been faithful to others, to ourselves, or to our God. We have not seen plainly enough the One we need most to see.

The longing is so rich. The hunger is so deep. The need is so vast. The pain is so great. "Whosoever," Jesus said. I am so glad for that word. For it is the only answer I know for people who want to find out whether or not the truth of God—the church of God—is indeed accepting of all. *Whosoever* is a word that calls out, rings clear, breaks through, shines forth, and gives life. It is a word to gladden the heart, set the captive free, make the blood run hot, quicken every pulse, and pity every groan. It is a word without conditions, qualifiers, or precursors. It is unrestricted, universal, undaunted, and unreserved.

The darkly radiant figure in the painting waits, with arms outstretched, both needing us and reaching out to our need. From a distance, the face is no more than mere shadows, and yet something within us cries out hallelujah, yes, and amen! As we approach, we can see the face plainly now and we know it. For in that face is seen everything that the world is looking for and more. In that face is found sweet redemption and release, reconciliation and fulfillment, validation and sanctuary, empowerment and life, faith, hope, and love. In that face is found embodied existence, same-gender acceptance, heterosexual affirmation, and all the shades in between, the celibate's preference, gender equality, a love supreme. Half-believer, inadequate believer, nonbeliever, or true believer, in that face is mirrored our own inner world. In that face is the whole of creation, the reflection of God's presence. In that face is the *imago Dei*, the joy of knowing ourselves. In that face is the promise of our interconnectedness as the rainbow people of God and with all of life. In that face and in that word and in that name is our model, our moral, and our imperative. Jesus says whosoever is welcome here. We are all of us one. That means you are accepted. I am accepted. We are accepted. All are accepted: all women and all men, all generations and all genders, all ethnicities and all nations, all colors and all cultures, all conditions and all convictions, all creeds and all communities—for all time. Whosoever. Come. Home. Ashé. Amen.

# 8

# I Think That's What It Takes

DEREK PENWELL

The Reverend Dr. Derek Penwell is an author, editor, speaker, and activist. He is the senior minister of Douglass Boulevard Christian Church (Disciples of Christ) in Louisville, Kentucky, and a lecturer at the University of Louisville in religious studies and humanities. He is the author of articles ranging from church history to aesthetic theory and the tragic emotions, as well as his first book, *The Mainliner's Survival Guide to the Post-Denominational World*. This sermon was preached as the Thirteenth Annual Matthew Shepard Sermon at Trinity Parish in Seattle, Washington, on Sunday, October 9, 2011.

---

*Matthew 22:1–14*

We gather here today to offer our worship to God. In the process, we also seek to commemorate the life of a gay man who was left to die alone. Thirteen years ago, two men took Matthew Shepard from a bar in an automobile, robbed him, pistol-whipped him, tortured him, and tied him to a fence to die alone in the night. He didn't die on the fence, because a passerby the next morning saw him. He died six days later in a hospital, on October 12, 1998—a victim of senseless violence against somebody on the margins.

That Matthew Shepard was gay apparently gave those two men all the motive they needed to inflict as much damage as their minds could concoct.

In the years since, Matthew Shepard has become a symbol of all that hatred can do when unleashed on the world.

A few years after he died, on a gray day in November 2000, when the sky looked like lead and the leaves had all vanished, I went to Creech Funeral Home in Middlesboro, Kentucky, down in Appalachia where I lived, to perform a funeral for Bryan Landon.

I didn't know Bryan; he'd spent most of his adult life up in Louisville, where he'd finally succumbed to the ravages of AIDS. My friend Bill, the funeral director, had asked me the day before if I'd perform the funeral, since Bryan didn't have a church home, and his family refused to provide assistance because they disapproved of his "lifestyle." I said I'd be glad to do what I could.

Bill said to me, "But I want you to know right off the bat that, because he was estranged from his family and his church, there might not be many folks there."

"Not a problem," I said.

But as I walked into the funeral home on that cold November day, it occurred to me that I'd not absorbed the full implications of Bill's warning. Not many people had shown up. And by "not many," I mean *nobody* had shown up. I waited in the chapel for five minutes or so after the funeral was supposed to have started.

Just Bryan Landon and me.

Finally, Bill came into the back of the chapel with someone I didn't know offhand. She sat in the back row. Bill made his way up front. And I said, "Oh, good. Is that a member of his family?"

"No," he said, "that's the woman who cleans for us."

I looked at him, puzzled. He said, "Well, in twenty-five years as a funeral director, I've never had a funeral where nobody showed up, and I figured somebody besides you and me ought to bear witness to this man's passing."

And so, on a gray November day in 2000, along with a funeral director and a cleaning woman, I buried Bryan Landon.

He died of AIDS. Nobody who knew him came to witness that he'd ever even walked this earth.

He had a family; he'd had friends along the way; he grew up in the Baptist church, singing "Jesus Loves the Little Children"—all the children

## Part Two: Calling for Liberation

of the world. But in the end, nobody came to claim him, to speak words over him, to call him a child of God. So, we three strangers wound up offering him up to God on the wings of weary and bedraggled prayers, clinging to all the hope we could muster in a gray place.

What continues to haunt me about that day is that I still cannot find words to express the sadness, the outrage, the terribleness of it all.

Where was the church for Bryan Landon?

Where's the church on this whole issue of our gay, lesbian, bisexual, or transgender sisters and brothers created by God? Who stands with them? Who stands up for them?

And what would it even look like to stand up?

I think that's the question raised by Matthew Shepard's death, by Bryan Landon's death.

What would it take for the church to make a difference in a world where people are bullied, killed, and abandoned for being who God created them to be? What would it take?

Jesus, in our Gospel text for today, has been in a long conversation with the chief priest and the elders of the temple. The occasion that prompted this conversation was the first act that Jesus performed after entering Jerusalem on a donkey, way back at the beginning of chapter 21.

Remember that? Jesus comes into Jerusalem, now a few days prior to his death, to the enthusiastic support of the people—who are convinced he's the Messiah, the long-awaited political/military leader who will lead a revolution to oust the Roman occupation.

That little parade makes the hairs on the back of the necks of the political leadership stand up.

His first act after entering to a chorus of Hosannas was to go straight to the temple and start turning over the tables of the money-changers, telling the folks in charge that they've destroyed God's house of prayer, they've made it a den of robbers.

Remember that?

What happens next, though, is the really telling part of the story. Jesus, it says in verse 14, after exposing as frauds the people entrusted with the caretaking of God's house, welcomes the blind and the lame to the temple, and he heals them.

Jesus calls out the big shots, and right under their noses receives with open arms the people those big shots have assiduously attempted to exclude.

This little jaunt into the temple makes the hairs on the back of the necks of the religious leadership stand up. In fact, they're so annoyed with Jesus that they buttonhole him the next day and ask him by what authority he's doing all this stuff. Just who does he think he is?

So Jesus launches into a series of parables to tell the religious leaders who he thinks he is and, perhaps just as importantly, who he doesn't think they are.

The parable of the wedding banquet is the third in this series, all keyed by, I would like to suggest, Jesus making a statement about who should be allowed into God's house—and what God thinks of the leaders who're supposed to be running things.

So our parable for today involves a king who's going to give a wedding banquet for his son. Each time the king sends out the wedding invitations, however, they're rudely declined. The king asks for the pleasure of his subjects' presence at a wonderful occasion, but they're preoccupied, tending to other things—things they're convinced are more important than whatever the king has in mind.

In an honor/shame-based culture like the one prevalent in the ancient Near East, this was the granddaddy of all social snubs. You don't turn down a king, then beat and kill the king's slaves!

This, of course, enrages the king. So what does he do? He invites in everybody else who wasn't important enough to get an invitation the first time around—both the good and the bad.

The king throws an enormous party for folks on the margins, welcoming all those people who are used to being left out of the important stuff, those who've been abused, pushed aside, excluded, those who've been bullied and abandoned to die alone.

You see, the kingdom of God does not exist where some are not welcome—where the lame and the blind, the tax collectors and prostitutes, the hungry and the poor stand on the outside looking in. The kingdom of God does not exist where people are barred entrance because of sexual orientation or gender identity, because of race or immigration status.

So how can we as a church tell people they're welcome?

People will finally know they're welcome not because we *advertise* our solidarity (as important as that is) but because we *show* them.

We keep throwing open the doors and inviting people to come in.

We keep working on behalf of those who've been turned away by the very people who are important enough to get invited to the party.

Part Two: Calling for Liberation

We keep standing side by side with those left to die alone.

What would it take for the church to accept the host's invitation to attend the party right alongside those who've systematically been told they're not welcome?

William J. Bausch gives us a glimpse of what it might look like, what I think it takes. Bausch relates the story of a man remembering the day he learned to hate racism—at the age of five:

> The walk home from school was only about five blocks. I usually walked with some friends. On this day I walked alone. Happy, but in a hurry, I decided to take the shortcut through the alley. Without a care in the world I careened around the corner. Then I looked up—too late to change course. I had walked into a back-alley beating. There were three big white kids. In retrospect they were probably no more than sixth graders, but they looked like giants from my kindergarten perspective.
>
> There was one black kid. He was standing against a garage, his hands behind his back. The three white kids were taking turns punching him. They laughed. He stood silently except for the involuntary groans that followed each blow. And now I was caught. One of the three grabbed me and stood me in front of their victim. "You take a turn," he said. "Hit the [expletive deleted]!" I stood paralyzed. "Hit him or you're next!" So I did. I feigned a punch. I can still feel the soft fuzz of that boy's turquoise sweater as my knuckles gently touched his stomach. I don't know how many punches there were. I don't know how long he had to stand backed up against that garage.
>
> After my minute participation in the conspiracy, they let me go and I ran. I ran home crying and sick to my stomach. I have never forgotten. Thirty-five years later that event still preaches a sermon to me every time I remember it. One can despise, decry, denounce, and deplore something without ever being willing to suffer, or even be inconvenienced, to bring about change.
>
> If there is one thing that Jesus taught us, it was how to suffer with and for others. Jesus walked the way of the cross. He taught us the meaning of suffering as a servant. Perhaps my first chance to follow that example came in the alley by a garage thirty-five years ago. I don't know if that black boy from the alley grew up, or where he lives, or what he does today. I never knew his name.
>
> I wish I did. I wish I could find him. I need to ask his forgiveness—not for the blow I delivered, for it was nothing, but for the

blows I refused to stand by his side and receive. I think that's what it takes.[1]

That's not easy. That's not get-up-and-go-to-church-on-Sunday-morning easy.

It's hard. I know. Standing up for people this culture doesn't think are worth it is hard, painful work.

But, as Father Daniel Berrigan once said, "If you want to follow Jesus, you'd better look good on wood."

You see, as a people who claim to follow a savior who was strapped to his own rough-cut piece of lumber and left to die alone, we can't stand idly by and watch the world do that to even one more person.

To Matthew Shepard. To Bryan Landon. To Jesus.

It's time for the rest of the children of God to stand by the side of those forgotten, abused, bullied, and left to die alone . . . even if it comes at a cost.

I think that's what it takes.

---

1. Bausch, *World of Stories*, 243–44.

# 9

## It's Harder to Be Us: The Gospel of Forgiveness for People on the Margins

### Sandhya Rani Jha

An ordained minister in the Christian Church (Disciples of Christ), the Reverend Sandhya Rani Jha currently serves as both the Director of the Oakland Peace Center and Director of Interfaith Programs for East Bay Housing Organizations in Oakland, California. She previously served as Senior Pastor of First Christian Church in Oakland and as Minister of Transformation and Reconciliation for the Christian Church (Disciples of Christ). Her publications include *Pre-Post-Racial America: Spiritual Stories from the Front Lines*. This sermon was originally preached at First Congregational Church of Oakland on April 27, 2014.

---

*John 20:19–31*

My mother's from Scotland, and there's an unofficial slogan there:
  *Here's tae us; wha's like us?*
  *Damn few an' they're aw deid.*
It roughly translates as "Here's to us! Who's like us? Damned few, and they're all dead."
  The thing I love about that slogan is that it's a slogan of survivors. It's the slogan of a people the English tried to wipe out and subjugate. It's the

slogan of a people who know they are exceptional, but it's tempered with "Don't get cocky."

You probably have friends who just celebrated Passover, and if you know the story of Passover, you'll see how it maps onto a similar saying in the Jewish community. A friend of mine had a sign hanging over her desk when we worked at The Interfaith Alliance. It read:

*A Summary of All Jewish Holidays:*
*They tried to kill us.*
*They didn't succeed.*
*Let's eat!*

The thing I love deeply about our city of Oakland is that it takes this theme to the next level: we're a city of survival and of speaking truth. We are a city of prophets. When there are systematic efforts to underpay and to sacrifice and to cause violence—economic or otherwise—to certain parts of our population, we say, "No!"

So why is it, then, that in our city of prophets, we are still only surviving, and we are not thriving?

There was a part of our Scripture that you may not have noticed in the reading this morning. Practically Jesus' first words to his disciples after the resurrection were these: "If you forgive the sins of any, they are forgiven them. If you retain the sins of any, they are retained" (John 20:23).

Frankly, if you ask me, it feels like Jesus is asking a lot.

After all, they may not have known all of the persecution that was ahead of them, but they certainly knew what had happened to Jesus. The resurrection was absolutely a miracle beyond comprehension, but for all of his practice of forgiveness, he was tortured and killed.

It was already hard enough following in his footsteps. It was already hard enough choosing a path that guaranteed being further marginalized. His death was a foretaste of the next four hundred years of risk and danger and violence that would befall his disciples. They were a people understandably living in fear. The resurrection was a miracle, and it changed everything, but even so everything still felt the same: the powers that had killed Jesus were still in charge of the day-to-day operations of this world. And now, on top of that, the disciples were asked to forgive those who would seek to harm and destroy them.

## Part Two: Calling for Liberation

It was harder being them than the people who opposed them.

༄

I'm standing in a room full of prophets this morning. First Congregational Church is a church that speaks truth to power. At a certain level, to be a Christian following the teachings of Christ, if you do it right (and I believe there is a way to do it right), means being a prophet, because you will ultimately be lifting up an alternative model of what it means to be community.

It's easy enough to say, "Forgive people." But it's not as easy to say it in this room.

It's not easy to say it to someone who has faced risk to safety and life, who has had love withheld from them simply because they are LGBTQ.

It's not easy to say it to someone whose community is under assault because the Prison Industrial Complex is systematically working to dehumanize, enslave, and kill black and brown men and women.

It's not easy to say it to someone who has escaped domestic or sexual violence.

Some of you know who Mel White is. About twenty years ago, he and his partner bought a home in Lynchburg, Virginia, so that they could be in the front row of Jerry Falwell's church every Sunday as a living embodiment of a God-blessed and God-loving gay couple worshiping the same God Jerry Falwell worshiped. He founded an organization called Soulforce, modeled on the nonviolent civil disobedience teachings of Jesus, Gandhi, and King, and took LGBTQ Christians and allies to denominational gatherings to stand up for LGBTQ inclusion in their policies, risking arrest every time. He also took those young LGBTQ youth to Liberty University and Bob Jones University as a living witness to God's love for all of God's children, and they faced regular harassment by those student bodies.

A couple of years ago, Mel White and his partner packed up the U-Haul and headed west to California. And I heard him say that in some ways he regretted the past twenty years. He regretted exposing good, decent, young LGBTQ people to so much ugliness and dehumanization during those campus visits and meetings with Jerry Falwell's church, and he was not certain it had made any difference.

I think about the fact that Brandy Martell was killed a mile from here for no reason other than being transgender.[1] I think about young Sasha's

---

1. Brandy Martell, a young black transgender woman, was sitting in her car on a

skirt being set on fire on an Oakland bus because Sasha wouldn't conform to a particular gender identity.[2]

And Jesus wants us who follow him to forgive.

It can be harder to be us.

※

I recently attended a Kingian Nonviolence training. Some of you know Kazu Haga, who leads these trainings. He often says nonviolence is a way of life, not a tactic. It is not something you switch on for the protest and then switch off for your day-to-day life. And if I might note, we're sometimes better at practicing nonviolence during the protest than in the strategy meetings. We're sometimes better at extending forgiveness to our opponents than to one another. Where nonviolence is often hardest to practice is in board meetings, in relationships, in family settings.

Rubin "Hurricane" Carter passed away last week. You may know him from either the movie or the Bob Dylan song about his life, or you may even remember his boxing career. He was arrested and jailed for a crime he didn't commit. He was black in the wrong place at the wrong time, and he fought until he was released. While in prison, he wouldn't wear the uniform, eat the food, or do the prison work. He knew he was not a prisoner and he refused to let them make him one.

Which made me think about today's Scripture passage about forgiveness. While I've always read this passage as Jesus placing yet another burden on us, another impossible standard to meet, is it possible Jesus was trying to make our lives on the margins easier? Was this Jesus' last act of mercy before ascending into heaven? Was he perhaps telling us not "it will be harder to be you; deal with it," but was he actually telling us, "You do not have to be prisoners?" Perhaps Jesus was actually giving to his beloved and faithful disciples power over the one thing they would always have control

---

Saturday night in downtown Oakland with her friends in May 2012. Some men approached the car and proceeded to flirt with her. She told them she was trans. They left and returned hours later with a gun and shot her at point-blank range, killing her instantly. Her parents insisted on burying her in a church service as a man, so her friends hosted a memorial service honoring her as Brandy, the woman they had known and loved. The memorial was held at the Oakland Peace Center.

2. Sasha Fleischman, an agender youth, fell asleep on a bus in Oakland in November 2013 and awoke on fire—another youth had set fire to the skirt being worn by Sasha. As a result, Sasha suffered severe burns and spent three weeks in the hospital burn unit.

over—their attitudes toward others. No matter the suffering they would endure for remaining faithful, no one could make them prisoners if they knew they had the power to forgive and chose to use it.

After all, there is liberation in forgiveness. It is a key to get out of the prison we have built for ourselves, a prison with walls of bitterness and bars of hatred. Imagine if Oakland were not only a city of prophets but also of grace—grace toward those in charge, sure . . . but grace toward each other. Imagine what a city we could be if we freed ourselves from the prison of withholding forgiveness.

I have a little firsthand experience with this. Many of you know I identify more with my South Asian heritage than my Scottish heritage. I knew my Indian family and grew up with them in my life. I did not grow up knowing my family in Scotland. In Britain in the 1960s, interracial and interreligious relationships were not accepted. My grandfather died not speaking to my mother because she was seeing my father. I think possibly to honor the legacy of her dead husband, my grandmother kept up that same lack of communication. When I was twelve, I sent her a snarky letter telling her she had missed out on a fantastic granddaughter. She wrote back, and eventually I visited her at the age of fifteen. It was awkward but we knew how to behave ourselves. When my father and I tricked my mother into visiting her mother for the first time in more than thirty years, it was the happiest day in my father's life—his lifelong regret was having broken the relationship between his wife and her family. To be sure, Scots are not known for their expressiveness, so my mother and I stood at the door of my grandmother's home in Glasgow and rang the bell. My grandmother opened the door and said, "Well, you've put on a bit of weight," which was her way of saying, "I'm sorry." And my mother said, "Right; nice to see you, too, Mum. What's for tea?" which was her way of saying, "I forgive you." When my grandmother died ten years ago, my mother and father were at her bedside. That exchange of "you've put on weight" and "what's for tea" offered my mother liberation that Robert the Bruce couldn't rival.

You are prophets, every one of you, whether you want to be or not. You are casting a vision of an alternative community, which is what prophets do, from the Hebrew Bible to Jesus to you. You are inheritors of a legacy of justice.

And that means the world will try to co-opt you or tear you down.

This community exists to put you back together again, to keep you whole, as broken as it sometimes is, so that you do not have to be a prophet alone.

But here is the message I believe Jesus was giving his disciples, his final liberating act, which I give to you also:

You are no one's prisoner.

You are a gloriously made child of God. Turn to your neighbor—let them know, "I am a gloriously made child of God." Now turn to that neighbor and tell them, "You are a gloriously made child of God."

As you fight for others to see themselves and each other as a gloriously made child of God, carry with you God's biggest promise to you, Jesus' liberating promise to you, and my promise to you with the confidence of our risen savior:

You will never be anyone's prisoner.

Amen.

# 10

# In Memory of Brandy Martell

## Tai Amri Spann-Wilson

Tai Amri Spann-Wilson was raised as a Quaker in South Jersey/Philadelphia and formerly served as copastor of the First Christian Church in Oakland, California. He earned a BA in writing and poetics from the Jack Kerouac School of Disembodied Poetics at Naropa University and attended the Pacific School of Religion. This sermon was preached at First Christian Church of Oakland on May 6, 2012, just a week after the murder of Brandy Martell, a transgender woman gunned down in Oakland. Brandy had declined advances made by flirtatious men, telling them she was transgender. They returned hours later and tragically shot her at point-blank range.

---

*Hebrews 12:1–3 · Ephesians 6:10–18*

(*In addition to Scripture readings, this sermon began with a reading of Langston Hughes' poem "Mother to Son." The speaker, a weary mother, begins by saying, "Well, son, I'll tell you: Life for me ain't been no crystal stair."*[1])

When Langston Hughes writes, "Life for me ain't been no crystal stair," I'm reminded of the popular black gospel song by the Reverend James

---

1. The full text of "Mother to Son" is available online. Copyright laws prevent us from publishing the entire poem in this collection.

Cleveland, "I Don't Feel No Ways Tired." For those of you who don't know the song, the chorus includes the line, "Nobody told me that the road would be easy; I don't believe He brought me this far to leave me."

But if I'm honest, the truth of the matter is that most times—especially times like these—I do feel so very, very tired. If I have the courage to admit it, I often feel like I've been brought this far but I just can't go any further. Sometimes I just want to sit down on those splintered steps described by Hughes, which seem to be the steps I encounter the most. Sometimes I just want to give in and give up; "Life for me ain't been no crystal stair."

Yet other times I feel like I just need to remember who I am, and if I could remember that I would be just fine. If I could just remember that I am good and holy and strong and worthy, I might be able to keep going, I might be able to do G-d's work. But when life unfolds in all its tragic complexity, as it frequently does, it seems so difficult to heed the call, to do all the things G-d is calling us to.[2]

I'm reminded of how difficult this calling is when the children I work with tell me that they're scared to walk through their front doors because of the gangs that haunt their front steps.

I'm reminded of how difficult this calling is when I'm walking down the street past a woman carrying on an incomprehensible conversation with herself.

I'm reminded of how difficult this calling is when I hear about people like Brandy Martell, who, as you likely know, was murdered last Sunday in downtown Oakland and might still be alive if she hadn't been transgender.

Sometimes I feel like Peter, James, and John in the garden with Jesus before he was arrested, failing to stay awake to pray with their Lord. Jesus looks at them knowingly and says, "The spirit indeed is willing, but the flesh is weak" (Matt 26:41). Even on the eve of the loss of their friend, brother, and savior, they found themselves just wanting to go to sleep—to not even have to try to face what was coming. Likewise, my flesh can feel so very weak, even when my spirit wants to break down all of the walls of injustice.

---

2. Editor's note: Hyphens are used in this manuscript intentionally, at the request of the preacher. Hyphenating the word *God* is a way to keep the name of God holy, similar to the way Jewish Scriptures render the most holy name of God as YHWH. Written as such (without vowels), the name of God is impossible to pronounce, which adds to its level of reverence. Later in this sermon, the word *kingdom* is likewise hyphenated, which serves as a way of talking about the realm of God announced by Jesus in nonhierarchical terms, implying kinship and mutuality.

So how can we stay awake through our pain to do the work of building G-d's kin-dom here on earth? How do we move toward the crystal stair, all without collapsing in exhaustion on stairs chock-full of tacks, splinters, and torn-up boards?

In Heb 12:1–3, the author encourages a local congregation by saying, "Therefore, since we are surrounded by so great a cloud of witnesses, let us also lay aside every weight and the sin that clings so closely, and let us run with perseverance the race that is set before us, looking to Jesus the pioneer and perfecter of our faith, who for the sake of the joy that was set before him endured the cross, disregarding its shame, and has taken his seat at the right hand of the throne of God. Consider him who endured such hostility against himself from sinners, so that you may not grow weary or lose heart." The sentiment here is that just as Jesus followed his calling and faced his fate even though he knew it would lead to his death—he refused to give in to death-dealing powers no matter the cost—so should we. But how are we supposed to do this? How *can* we do this?

Once again I look to the Scriptures, this time to the book of Ephesians, where Paul writes to a congregation about their struggles and reminds them that their struggles are not against other human beings but against those things unseen, "the cosmic powers of this present darkness." Paul writes that in the face of such struggles, we should "*stand.*" We should *stand* with "the belt of truth around [our] waist"; we should *stand* with "the breastplate of righteousness" over our shoulders; we should *stand*, wearing shoes that will make us ready "to proclaim the gospel of peace" (Eph 6:12–15).

In the face of adversity, Paul says, we stand with the belt of truth around our waist and the breastplate of righteousness over our shoulders, all in order to proclaim the message of G-d's truth and righteousness, which is nothing other than the message of peace.

Through standing tall in the truth of G-d's love, by protecting our hearts with that which is right, by making sure that our feet carry us on the mission to spread G-d's peace, love, and justice, by protecting our minds with G-d's salvation, by slicing through lies of injustice and oppression with the sword of the Spirit, and, perhaps most importantly, by praying on every occasion, we stand. We become ambassadors for peace.

As people of faith, as people on the margins, as people who long for peace and love and justice:

We stand, together.

We don't turn back.

## In Memory of Brandy Martell · Spann-Wilson

We do not sit down on the splintered steps.
We do not fall.
We keep on going.
We keep on climbing.
We share and embody the gospel of peace.

"Nobody told me that the road would be easy; [but] I don't believe He brought me this far to leave me."

# 11

## All of You

### Meredith Guest

After completing a BA in religion and philosophy, the Reverend Meredith Guest continued studying philosophy at the University of Southern Mississippi and then attended the Southern Baptist Theological Seminary. Her time as a Southern Baptist minister was brief, however, in large part due to matters of conscience. She is the author of *Son, I Like Your Dress*, a memoir about her transition from male to female gender identity.

---

*Romans 12:2*

Like most male-to-female transsexuals, when I first came out, I wanted to purge my life of anything and everything that had to do with being a man, and I did everything I could to change myself into that idealized image I carried around in my head of what I thought it meant to be a woman. Every article of clothing I bought during this period either was pink or had pink in it. I even bought pink jeans, which are not easy to find, especially in my size.

    Now, I live on a little ranch, and I had horses at the time. If you know anything about horses, you know that if you get within ten feet of one, you invariably end up with mud and manure on you, so pink jeans made no sense. And besides, I don't look very good in pink.

But it didn't matter. I didn't want anyone mistaking me for a man.

One day I was out working on the property. Since I was never pretty enough to find a man to do the weed-eating while I did something domestic and demur, like cleaning his hairs out of the bathroom sink, I was wearing my leather riding chaps over my pink jeans in order to protect my legs. On a break, I decided to go up and get the mail out of the box just up the road. When I looked to see if any cars were coming, I saw a sheriff's car pull into the intersection a long stone's throw away, but since it looked like he was going to go straight, I turned away and stepped onto the road. A couple of seconds later, the sheriff's car pulled up beside me, and when I looked over, I saw that he had rolled down his window and was laughing his head off. "From down there," he said to me, "it looked like you didn't have anything on under your chaps!" We both had a great laugh. Needless to say, I never wore my pink jeans with my chaps after that.

I also—in as much as it was possible—cut all ties with those who had known me before. I wanted to be around people who only knew Meredith. It's one of the things I liked about the Unitarian Universalist church in town. Not only did they accept me, no one there had ever known me when I was doing my stellar impersonation of a man.

One Sunday after worship, not too long after I'd been going to this church, my good friend Jodi said, "Let's go to the women's group meeting this week."

"Really?" I asked skeptically.

"Sure. Come over to my house on Thursday, and we'll walk to Jean's together."

Now Jodi was the first female friend I had after I came out, and I was completely infatuated with having a girlfriend as a girl. I felt all of about fifteen—in a fifty-year-old body. So, naturally, I agreed.

The next day I got an email from the group leader informing me that the topic of that week's women's group meeting was childhood, and everyone was to bring a photo of herself at about age twelve. (Jodi swears she did not know this when she invited me!) In a classic case of what a friend of mine calls "the staff work of omnipotence," a couple of weeks earlier I had unexpectedly received a package from my mom full of childhood photos. "I thought you should have these now," the note inside said. Guess what was in there: a lovely 4 × 6 photo of twelve-year-old Hank. Who says God doesn't have a sense of humor?

To my credit, I went to the women's group, and as each of the women shared, she placed a photo of herself as a little girl on the table, the kind of little girl I had always longed to be. And then it was my turn. Their response to my photo was, of course, wonderful. In fact, they were fascinated.

On the way back to Jodi's house, I told her how hard that had been for me. How I had dreaded it all week. How I didn't want any of them to know about my past. How I wanted them to know only me as Meredith, not Hank. Just then Jodi stopped, took my hand in hers, looked into my eyes and said, "Mer, we want all of you. All of you."

I'm telling you this because isn't this what God is constantly saying to each of us? "I want all of you." And don't you have things in your life you would like to get rid of—things you can't accept, things you would like to forget, things about which you feel ashamed or guilty or embarrassed? I'm not alone here. I am not the only one here with a past, am I?

Now, sometimes we call these things that we would like to get rid of "sin," and sometimes they are, because sin is whatever separates us from God, from others, and from our true selves. Addictions are sin, especially those addictions that are unrecognized, unnamed, and unclaimed. At 4.5 percent of the world's population, the U.S. consumes roughly a fourth of the world's energy, making us what might reasonably be described as energy drunks. And take a look in our garages, our attics, our pantries, and especially our children's bedrooms and the evidence is undeniable that we are all hooked on a constant flow of stuff pouring from the teat of the corporate cow. These addictions anesthetize us and thereby alienate us from our true selves as well as from a huge part of the human family that must do with too little because we have too much. And these addictions, like all addictions, come at great cost. Unless and until we acknowledge these things as sin, confess and repent, one day people may look back and say of us what Jesus said—that we were a people who gained the world yet lost our souls.

But sometimes what we call sins are actually symptoms, because most sins, if not all, arise from unhealed wounds. By now we all know that there are wounds we carry deep within us, often from childhood, that, for one reason or another, have never been healed, and that these wounds can create all manner of havoc in our lives. But again, as with our addictions, I think there are wounds we rarely recognize: the loss of community, work driven by necessity but devoid of desire or pleasure or meaning, a persistent sense of powerlessness, alienation from the very earth on which we depend for life. All of these are wounds that desperately need to be healed, but healing is hard work, because first I have to acknowledge that I am wounded, and then I have to bring my wound up out of the darkness, often the darkness of unconsciousness, into the light where not only I but others, too, can see it clearly, and this always takes great courage. Nor can healing take place in the safety of our closets. Safely hidden away in my closet, I knew God accepted me as I was. Years before I came out, I knew I was not bad, not evil nor wrong nor perverted. In fact, I had come to truly believe that God made me the way I was for some purpose. Theologically, I had it right, but it was only when I felt the touch of another person's hand, only when I looked into her eyes and heard her say those words—we want all of you—that I could actually begin to believe it. That's the meaning of incarnation. The word must still become flesh.

But as important as confession, repentance, and healing are—and they are important—they are not the *telos* of the Christian life, which is to say, they are not the end point, the goal, the purpose. Rather, they are prerequisites for something that is at one and the same time both wonderful and terrible, something too good to be true and too true to be good.

Let me give you an illustration of what I'm talking about. I am fortunate to have a building on our property that has a space suitable for movement, and improvisational movement has been an important part of my spiritual practice for years. For a series of weeks some time back, a small group of us gathered at my place to do movement together, and one night after we'd been doing it for a while, I introduced moving with the bodkin. A bodkin is a short, stylized wooden sword. In addition to being beautiful, a bodkin is heavy. I turned on a light at one end of the room, so that whoever was moving with the bodkin could also move with their shadow on the opposite wall. (We divided the room to avoid someone getting some accidental whacking, because you really don't want to get whacked with this thing.) I then gave the bodkin to a woman I will call Sharon.

At first, Sharon wasn't so sure about moving with this thing that looked a lot like a weapon. "Oh, I'm not so sure I want to do this," she said. To which I replied, "Okay, but why don't you give it a try, and if you don't feel comfortable, put it down and someone else can try it." She reluctantly agreed. I put on a piece of music, and she started moving, clearly uncertain about the whole thing. I went on to lead some other movements, but toward the end of the piece, I looked over to see how Sharon was doing. She was standing with her legs apart, and the bodkin thrust upward above her in a classic stance of triumph. In the sharing afterward, I asked how it had felt, and Sharon reported with no reluctance at all, "I felt powerful!" (And she looked powerful, too.) In fact, she looked completely transformed.

This is precisely what God is inviting us into—transformation—and it is both wonderful and terrible, too good to be true and too true to be good; for you see, Sharon never came back to movement. In fact, I don't think I ever heard from her again, and so I don't know why she never returned. But if I were to speculate, I'd say it had something to do with how Sharon saw herself. From what I had seen in previous groups and what I previously knew about Sharon, being powerful was at odds with the narrative she told herself and others about who she was, and so claiming power would have required letting go of the old, familiar story she had been constructing since childhood, then finding and creating an entirely new understanding of who she really was. That is no small task, and no part of her life would have been untouched: her marriage, her friendships, her work, her place in her family, her dysfunctional, codependent relationship with her grown daughter. Everything would have been up for grabs. So you see, finding, feeling, and claiming her power—while a wonderful experience for Sharon at the time—also held potentially terrible implications for her life as she had known it.

Instead of transformation what we often opt for is self-improvement, which is not necessarily a bad thing. The people who know me well—those who work with me and especially those who live with me—would no doubt welcome some self-improvement on my part and could, I'm sure, suggest several places where I might want to begin.

But don't you see? Self-improvement was what I was trying to do in eliminating my masculinity and turning myself into the most believable version of a woman I could. And to that end I shed more than a few units of blood, sweat, and tears—not to mention tens of thousands of dollars. But remember the Bible verse for the day, the passage from Romans in which Paul exhorts us to "not be conformed to this world, but be transformed by the renewing of your minds"? God didn't want to improve me. To God, I didn't need improving; I just needed to be transformed into my true self, and that would include all of me. Nothing would need to be left behind, eliminated, or burned on the altar of societal acceptance.

For those who wish to be the body of Christ, confessing our sins, repenting, and being healed are a vital part of a process that leads toward transformation. But transformation into what? Into being, like Jesus, the companions of God, and that, quite literally, scares the hell out of us—and for good reason. Like Jesus, we are invited to be visible incarnations of God's love, God's mercy, God's judgment, God's truth, God's compassion. God does not call us to improve ourselves. God calls us to be transformed, and this call to transformation is not about eliminating those parts of us that do not conform to some norm but placing all of who we are into the loving hands of God and trusting God to use it—all of it—in building the kin-dom of God.

Jodi's five words—"We want all of you"—changed my life as much as if someone had said to me, "You have won the lottery." And when we get this, when we really get it that God wants all of us, we will have won the lottery—and more.

# 12

## Dogs of Canaan

CHRISTIAN PIATT

Christian Piatt is the author of *postChristian* (2014), *Blood Doctrine* (2014), and *PregMANcy* (2012), and is the creator and editor of the "Banned Questions" book series. He writes for Patheos, *Huffington Post*, *Sojourners*, and others, and he serves as the Director of Author Development and Acquisitions for www.CrowdScribed.com. He can be found online at www.ChristianPiatt.com.

---

*Matthew 15:21–28*

My wife Amy and I try to make a point of having a date night once a week. But with two kids and a church to care for, that doesn't always happen. Last Friday was the first time in a month we had gone out as grown-ups, so we wanted to make it special.

Amy had been trying to get a reservation at Nostrana for months. Every time we found out we had a Friday evening free and secured a sitter, they were booked solid until after nine thirty. Might work for single hipsters, but not for a married guy whose two children would be begging for cereal and cartoons at the crack of dawn the next morning. But last week, we had three days' notice that our sitter was free, so Amy jumped online and reserved a table.

The reservation was for eight o'clock, but we showed up an hour early. The hostess suggested the bar across the street as a fun distraction until our table was free. It was called Crush.

"Looks really nice," I said, peering through the window.

"It's great," she smiled. "You'll love it." As we were halfway out the door, she added, "Oh, it's a gay bar, by the way."

Ah.

I felt like a character on *Seinfeld*. I was sure my surprise was obvious, but I felt like I needed to qualify it with something like, "Not that there's anything wrong with that." Who cares, right? A drink is a drink, and I've been in gay bars before. Heck, I once sang "Happy Birthday" to my wife in the style of Elvis before a drag show in Fort Worth, Texas.

So why was I nervous?

It was because I was going into an environment where I was, for once, the "other." Would they accept me? Would they spot me and judge me for invading their turf? Would somebody try and buy me a drink when Amy slipped off to the restroom? (Unfortunately, no luck on that last one. But hey, a guy can hope.)

The point is that I was the outsider, which is a pretty unfamiliar experience for a middle-class straight white guy. The extent of my otherness is generally limited to the fact that I'm left-handed (and a Christian living in Portland!).

I was okay with them, but would they be okay with me? Would I be accepted? Tolerated? Singled out? Judged?

Oh, to have such privilege, to have to go out of my way to find a place where I might be judged, simply for who I am.

I've heard a number of interpretations of what's going on in this Scripture passage from Matthew, but it's hard to get around the fact that Jesus comes off as kind of a jerk. Obviously, the author of this passage felt there was something important for us to get from this awkward exchange between Jesus and the Canaanite woman, but what is it?

Some folks suggest that Jesus had planned to honor her request for healing from the beginning but that he wanted to test her resolve first. So I guess she passed the test, persisting after being called a dog.

I've also heard some suggest that, because the only dogs who would have been allowed to scrounge under a table were little puppies, Jesus was using the word *dog* as a sort of term of endearment.

Can I get a quick show of hands from all of the women who can identify any derivation of the word *dog* that they would consider complimentary if it were applied to them? Anyone? Bueller?

There's another explanation that makes the most sense to me, but some folks are uncomfortable with it. What if Jesus was caught up in an utterly human moment of cultural bias? It would have been very common for Jews to refer to Canaanite Gentiles as dogs, or to use some other equally denigrating term. It wouldn't have been any more offensive than calling a gay person a "faggot" or a black person a "nigger" not so very long ago in our own contemporary history.

Now, you say those words and it gets a little bit uncomfortable, doesn't it? Because we know better . . . right?

All kinds of behaviors become normalized in a culture that deems it necessary for things to function the way the majority in power want them to. Women are denied the right to vote. Children work seventy-hour weeks in factories. People are forced into camps because they look too Asian. Folks are profiled in airports, in the workplace, or even in their own car for being a little too brown. Couples are denied equal caregiver rights, medical and insurance benefits, or even government tax status because of who they love.

Good thing we know better, right?

We'll get back to Jesus, but I want to leave him on the hook for another couple of minutes.

⚜

My friend Shannon is gay. He was born and raised in North Carolina, where such things simply didn't happen, and if they did, well, certainly no one ever talked about it. Shannon told me one time about how his dad had gotten frustrated by his lack of interest in sports, so he went out and bought him a go-kart to "man him up" a little. He left it covered by a tarp in the back of his truck, and then sent Shannon out to the truck on some fictitious errand to surprise him with the gift.

Instead, Shannon came back empty-handed. "All I found was some big lawnmower in the truck," he said.

"My dad should have known then," Shannon told me, "and maybe he did, deep down inside. But he never mentioned it, and neither did I."

As time went by, Shannon realized he was being called into ministry. I actually met him when he and Amy were classmates at Brite Divinity School in Fort Worth. I think he actually passed her a note during class asking to be her friend. The rest is history, of course. We've been close ever since. He's "Uncle Shannon" to our kids, and he was one of the only people—and certainly the only other male—present at the birth of our son, Mattias.

Shannon went through the entire three and a half years of graduate school, earning stellar grades and accolades for both his musical ability and his preaching skill along the way. He served as the music minister at a Disciples of Christ church in Weatherford, just west of Fort Worth. For some perspective, if Texas is the heart of the Bible Belt, and if Dallas-Fort Worth is the buckle of the Bible Belt, then Weatherford could easily qualify as the rhinestone on that buckle.

Despite the unlikely combination, Shannon has served at that church for a dozen years. They love him for who he is, though plenty of folks in the congregation probably struggle with the "gay issue." But for them, Shannon isn't an issue; he's family. And you love family, period.

But it's more complicated than that. The denomination has an ordination process that ministers go through after seminary. Once ordained, a minister can circulate their papers nationally in search of work. Without it, prospects are severely limited. And unfortunately, the area in Texas where Shannon works and went to seminary doesn't ordain people who are openly gay.

There are loopholes, as is the case in a lot of systems. He could have been ordained through the United Church of Christ, our sister denomination, which welcomes gay and lesbian clergy. Once ordained there, his status as clergy would be recognized by our denomination. He could have simply not brought it up during his ordination interviews; he likely would have squeaked through. In fact, some folks on the ordination committee who knew him and his sexual orientation encouraged him to keep quiet about it.

But although a straight person may not think about their sexuality in the context of ministry, that's actually a privilege a lot of people don't have. Let me offer a more benign example. How many right-handed people here think about being right-handed on a daily basis? Now, how about my sinister-handed friends?

The reason we lefties think about being left-handed more than the rest of you think about being right-handed is that the world is built for right-handed people. You just don't recognize it because the privilege is invisible to you.

Until you don't have it, that is.

So Shannon was forced to sublimate a part of himself that had been used to deny him equality at the moment when he's asked about his call to ministry, and about why he feels the need to answer a call to reach out to the disempowered, the marginalized, the other, the less than.

Shannon sees his sexuality as a defining trait of his ministry, one that he can't simply set aside and ignore when expedient, or when those in power—those with privilege they don't even recognize having, those who would just as soon call him a dog—tell him to be less than honest about who he is.

And for that, he was denied ordination.

More than a decade later, while still serving the same congregation in Texas where he's been since seminary, Shannon reentered the ordination process. His region still won't ordain him, but the Northern California-Nevada region has welcomed his request. He has to fly from Dallas to San Francisco several times to interview with them because he can't do it in the very community he serves.

Some people have been asking Shannon, "Why now, after all of these years? And why California?" To which he shared the following letter online:

> Some people have asked about my recent post concerning ordination. So, here's what's going on.
>
> To begin, I am gay.
>
> If this is a shock to you, I'm sorry—I thought we had met. If this is embarrassing to you, please know that I have carried that shame on your behalf my whole life, and I can't do it anymore. If this is uncomfortable for you, be aware I have shouldered that burden for you my whole life, and I can't do it anymore. If you think I am going to hell, please know that I am a Christian, that I am a minister, and that I am good with God. If you don't give a rip about my sexual orientation, thank you!
>
> That said, the region where I serve in ministry does not ordain openly gay people, and so I was never ordained after I graduated from seminary. I have served as a licensed minister these past eleven or so years. Going through the ordination process without being able to freely discuss my sexual orientation, and how it impacts my ministry, just did not seem right to me.

Therefore, I have applied for and been accepted into the ordination process in the Northern California-Nevada region, which was the reason for my recent trip to San Francisco. The meeting went very well, and hopefully I will be able to be ordained within the next year.

Central Christian Church in Weatherford, Texas, is my sponsoring congregation (I have been out to them for several years). They have been, and continue to be, unbelievably loving and supportive of my ministry and my life. As have many other colleagues and friends—and I thank you for that.

I am grateful to every person and circumstance that has made me the person I am today. As I prepare to hit the "post" button on this status, I do so anticipating a great release from fear and anxiety. Ladies and gentlemen, I present to you: me.

Peace,
Shannon

It wasn't shocking or remarkable that Jesus said what he did, at least not at the time to those witnessing. What was remarkable was that the woman persisted in her faith, and that it was her faith that overwhelmed existing cultural bias in the name of love and compassion—perhaps reminding Jesus that the heart of the Jewish tradition is love and compassion, extended to others, which of course became also the heart of Jesus' ministry.

You might say that it wasn't remarkable that a bus driver asked Rosa Parks to get out of her seat for a white man. Yet it was remarkable that she refused, and out of her courageous resistance a movement was born that forever changed the course of American history.

In the same way, it's not exactly surprising that a church region in Texas still refuses to ordain one of its most gifted and dedicated servants. What's incredible is that, despite the rejection, despite years of doubt and heartbreak, he has continued to pursue his call.

Will his story become part of history? Will it become a defining moment we'll look back on someday and say, "Right there—that's when it all changed"?

Maybe—maybe not. But we don't do such things to make history. We do them because the gospel compels us. We do them because we know in our hearts that it's right. We do them to liberate ourselves and others. We do them in the name of Love.

*Part Three*

Calling for Hospitality

# 13

## All Are Welcome?

### Nancy Steeves

The Reverend Dr. Nancy Steeves was ordained by the Presbyterian Church in Canada. After five years in parish ministry, experiencing the church to be an inhospitable place for sexual minorities, Nancy left ministry to practice law. She returned to her vocation with the United Church of Canada in 1998 and has been in team ministry with Southminster-Steinhauer United Church in Edmonton, Alberta, since 2003. This congregation became the first affirming ministry of the United Church of Canada in Alberta in 1999 and has mentored many other congregations on their affirming journeys. Nancy is an advocate for justice and a prophetic voice for honoring diversity. She received her Doctor of Ministry in Preaching from Chicago Theological Seminary in 2009.

---

*Luke 4:16–32*

I'm sure the synagogue in Nazareth must have had one of those wayside signs. You know the ones I mean. It would have had the name of the synagogue nicely hand-lettered on it along with the name of the rabbi, the time of the service on Shabbat, some slogan that made them sound inviting, and then the usual words in big letters: *"All Are Welcome!"*

Nazareth was a small community in the first century, with likely not more than a few hundred residents. We'd expect to find a warm welcome in the pews that day when their hometown boy turned up.

Word was getting around about their boy. They must have been bursting their buttons with pride when he got up to read Scripture (after all, in the congregation I grew up in, if you were male and had a strong reading voice that was enough to make you a candidate for ministry!). I suppose it might not have been that dissimilar for rabbinical candidates from small synagogues in the first century. Can you imagine the whispers as Jesus returned to his seat?

"Just listen to Mary's boy, doesn't he read well?"

"That son of Joseph is sure making a name for himself around Galilee!"

As the story goes, when he sat down, every eye in the place was on him—and that's when he blew it.

*If only Jesus had remained silent.* If only he had smiled and nodded. But somehow Jesus knew that there comes a time in each of our lives:

When silence is no longer faithful . . .

When there are those for whom we must raise our voice . . .

Those with whom we must cast our lot . . .

So Jesus had to tell them that while it was nice of them to welcome him home, he had really come to address those who weren't there to welcome him. He had come to address the brokenhearted:

The ones who had been left out . . .

The ones who were so painfully aware of their difference . . .

The ones imprisoned within themselves or within the systems that confined them . . .

The ones oppressed by their religion, their clergy, their emperor.

He came to the ones who weren't welcome in the synagogue, who weren't welcome to share a table. He came to those who had to leave home, didn't have a place to call home, couldn't go home, never had a home!

Sure, there must have been liberal, open-minded folk sitting in the synagogue that day. But even the open-minded began to sing a different tune: "Now look here, Joseph's boy . . . mind your mouth . . . don't let your mama hear you talking like this . . . the people just aren't quite ready for your message yet."

And they were filled with so much rage that they ran him out of town. It's really a story of welcome gone bad. Really, really bad.

Jesus' commitment to radical hospitality was one of the things that got him kicked out of town. And it was one of the things that got him killed.

He refused to live within the segregated lines that both the empire and his religious authorities had drawn. He insisted on eating with tax collectors and sinners. He touched lepers. He talked to women. He treated Samaritans—the heretics of his people—with dignity and respect. He accepted the wisdom of a Canaanite woman who persuaded him to get over his own tribalism and ethnocentricity and pay attention to hurting Gentiles, too. He took children in his arms and said we need to be like them. (Children were not prized creatures in the Roman Empire of the first century. They were social liabilities, a drain on scarce resources.) Jesus went home with guys like Zacchaeus, the despised and rejected collaborators of the Roman occupation. Over and over, everywhere he went, he refused to live within the boundaries prescribed by the purity laws and the social norms of his time. Over and over, he tried to erase the dividing lines, break down the dividing walls, and heal social divisions.

To be a community that meets in the name of Jesus of Nazareth is not about being liberal or conservative, evangelical or mainline, right-wing or left-wing. If we truly want to meet and greet one another in the name of Jesus, we'd better be about holy hospitality. Radical hospitality. For to follow Jesus as our wisdom teacher is to live into communities of *belonging*, not places of *welcome*. And there's a big difference.

Churches announcing that "all are welcome" are a dime a dozen. I was serving one of them in 1983. Two years earlier I had been welcomed into the vocation of ministry within the Presbyterian Church in Canada. The hometown crowd of my presbytery had laid their hands on me and sent me off with their blessing. The sign on the church where I was ordained said, "All Are Welcome." The sign on the church I was appointed to serve said, "All Are Welcome." The sign on the church where my presbytery conducted a hearing into my fitness for ministry, not because of my ethics, values, or beliefs but because of who and how I loved, also had a sign outside that said, "All Are Welcome."

Like so many other gay and lesbian clergy and parishioners, I came to know those words to mean that I am welcome . . . to live a lie.

I am welcome . . . to hide a piece of my identity.

I am welcome . . . to the club of "don't ask and don't tell."

I am welcome . . . to watch other couples get married.

I am welcome . . . to pretend I have a roommate.

## Part Three: Calling for Hospitality

And I am welcome to get out of Dodge if I speak my truth—or the masquerade comes to an end—or the wrong person discovers the truth of my life.

Every church likes to say, "All Are Welcome," but many of us have had good reason to discover these words actually mean "Some Are Welcome":

Some are welcome to get married here . . .

Some are welcome to be our leaders . . .

Some are welcome to teach our children . . .

Some are welcome to lead our youth . . .

Because belonging has its boundaries.

In a liberal democracy like Canada, we like to think that sexuality is no big deal in the twenty-first century. We like to think that our government and our churches, our friends and our coworkers, have no business knowing what two consenting adults share in private. But I want to tell you that for some, sexuality is a matter of exile or embrace, of belonging or longing to belong, of rejection or affirmation, of finding home or remaining homeless, of being known or remaining anonymous, of experiencing faith in isolation or in community. Those of us who are of a minority sexual orientation or gender identity bear many scars, and we need more than your welcome. We need affirmation: places and spaces that affirm our dignity, our value, our worth, that are safe for us not just to be but to belong; we need community with those who are not afraid to advocate for us and with us.

We have lots of welcoming churches; we even have a fair number of open-minded churches. But where are the brokenhearted churches? Isn't that the kind of community Jesus spoke of in Nazareth: the community of the brokenhearted for the brokenhearted? It's the kind of community where compassion has a complete anatomy: heart and mind, hands and feet, eyes and ears. To be that kind of community is to be a community of faith where we have not just an open door and an open mind but an open heart, a heart willing to let itself be broken by hearing hard stories, by receiving those who have been most fractured and broken by life. It means moving out of our own particular margins and our own particular oppressions to open our hearts to those whose hurts are very different than our own. It means living with our hearts wide open, broken open as bread is broken to be shared. It means making a safe home for all who are weary of their anonymous journeys. It means building a community where it is safe to know and to be known—where all really means all—where all are truly welcome to be and to belong.

# 14

## The Doctrine of Original Fabulousness

### Stephanie Spellers

The Reverend Canon Stephanie Spellers serves as the Canon for Missional Vitality in the Diocese of Long Island and teaches on mission at General Theological Seminary in New York City. A prolific writer, speaker, and consultant, she is the author of *The Episcopal Way* (with Eric Law) and *Radical Welcome: Embracing God, The Other and the Spirit of Transformation*. She served as founding priest for The Crossing, an emergent congregation based at the Cathedral of St. Paul in Boston. This sermon was originally preached at the Cathedral on May 6, 2007.

---

*John 13:33–35*

It's a blessing to be out on the road, sharing the gospel of Jesus Christ and the good news of radical welcome. It's a joy to tell stories of communities that are prayerfully learning to welcome and celebrate the power, gifts, and presence of the very people who have been systemically oppressed and cast to the margins of church and society: homeless and poor folks, children and young people, gay and lesbian and bisexual and transgender people, people of color.

It's also a blessing to bring that message home. You know and I know this Cathedral community is not perfect. We haven't "arrived" by any means—nobody has, at least not this side of heaven. But I see the Holy

## Part Three: Calling for Hospitality

Spirit working her way, moving us to take halting steps toward one another and toward our neighbors. I see you becoming a community that seriously lives the new commandment Jesus laid out in today's gospel: we want to love one another as Christ loved us, to love like the God who radically welcomed us all in the first place.

If there's a hitch—the distance most of us still have to travel—it's only partly about loving the Other. For this wisdom, I turn to drag queen, TV star, and pop diva RuPaul. For decades, he's told people, "Honey, if you can't love yourself, how the hell you gonna love somebody else?" This Sunday, I need to stand right beside my wise, elder queen and ask, "If you don't know yourself as beloved of God, how the hell you gonna share God's love with somebody else?"

RuPaul is 100 percent right: how can any of us offer the abundant, radiant, radical, unconditional love and welcome of God to somebody else, if we haven't first received the abundant, radiant, radical, unconditional love and welcome of God? You've got to be beloved if you're gonna be loving. Everything starts there.

I don't know why it's so hard to accept God's radical love for us; I only know that it is. Presiding Bishop Katharine Jefferts Schori spoke this week to hundreds of Episcopal clergy here in Massachusetts, and she told us the world desperately needs to hear the good news that we are all beloved of God. She asked us to find, celebrate, and bless the giftedness in other people, to make that radical affirmation our starting place.

One priest—a good friend of mine—had so much trouble with this concept that he finally jumped to his feet and asked her, "But what about original sin? What about the cross? Surely you can't build a faith with any integrity if you start with the assumption that everybody is made in the image of God, that everybody is beloved and gifted?" He couldn't take it. Clearly, he thought she was selling ChristianityLite, and he wasn't buying it.

I actually found myself hurting for him. I wanted to turn to him and say, "My brother, we know the doctrine of Original Sin, and it has its place. Maybe we also need to learn and live the doctrine of Original Fabulousness. Maybe we need to get rooted in what it means to be beloved, gifted, received, and held in the hands and eyes of God."

Creation itself is a result of the outpouring—the overflowing bounty—of God's love. And we? We are creations made in the image of our Creator. We are made from love and made to love. We will surely falter—the Scriptures are one story after another of that faltering—but every time we rise back up and extend love to another, we extend it to God, and open ourselves to receive more of God's love. This is what we were made for: to love and be loved. To be the beloved.

Yet we are so often tempted to doubt this truth about ourselves.

Why do we doubt it? I imagine it seems arrogant and even dangerous to elevate ourselves and say we're beloved. Somehow, it's a little too close to declaring we're perfect. But, you know, God's love has no correlation with our perfection. God's love is all about God's grace, and grace doesn't depend on you. Grace receives you: warts, thorns, faults, and everything else you judge and hate in yourself. Grace declares it all beloved. Not perfect, but precious, redeemable . . . beloved.

It's also tempting to doubt the good news of our belovedness because it's so hard to let anybody love us. I find it infinitely easier to focus on loving someone else. Then I'm in control. Then I don't need to open my heart and admit how desperately I want to be loved. And then I don't need to risk the utter terror of being rejected by the very one whose love I crave. (And although I'm using "I" statements, others of you here know what I'm talking about.)

If you're with me, try this experiment: let yourself open to the love of God. Try believing that God isn't going to reject you—not now, not ever. Paul said it in Romans: "Neither death, nor life, nor angels, nor rulers, nor things present, nor things to come, nor powers, nor height, nor depth, nor anything else in all creation, will be able to separate us from the love of God in Christ Jesus our Lord" (8:38–39). You may feel distant. You may think you've walked too far from God, but God never gives up on you, never closes her arms against you, never turns her back when you come running up the street, no matter what you're running from. It simply will not happen.

Can you let yourself be loved by the One whose love knows no limit? Close your eyes and let yourself hear it. For the next minute, we're going to pause. You'll hear me ringing the bell, and each time just repeat to yourself, "You are my beloved. I am so pleased with you . . . You are my beloved. I am so pleased with you . . ."

Don't doubt it for a moment. You are the Beloved. You are the Beloved. God is pleased with you. It's worth the effort to chant God's words like a mantra. Because that kind of love unleashes something powerful in us all. If I know I have the unconditional love of God, then I am dangerously free to love and surrender everything for Christ. I am free enough to be generous and daring in offering love and welcome to others, because I know that their presence isn't going to equal less love for me. I can go to the scariest place in the world, because I know I am wrapped in the love of the One who made the world.

Once you feel confident of your own belovedness, your own fabulousness, you can get out there and discover and celebrate and protect somebody else's fabulousness, especially in the people and cultures and places that our society has declared least gifted. I'm talking about the hordes of teens who run the streets just around the block every school day, the marginalized people living with HIV and AIDS in Africa and in Roxbury, the Other who sits next to you in the pew or stands near you during coffee hour, but whose story you do not know.

If I can see myself as beloved, then maybe I can extend that to you. Maybe we can draw out each other's stories, each other's gifts, each other's belovedness. We can make even more room in this very community for different gifts, different ways of leading, different ways of singing and celebrating.

You are beloved. It's time to believe it, and then spread it around. Alleluia and amen!

# 15

## Water on a Desert Road

BARBARA K. LUNDBLAD

The Reverend Dr. Barbara K. Lundblad is the distinguished Joe R. Engle Professor of Preaching Emerita at Union Theological Seminary in the City of New York. An ordained minister in the Evangelical Lutheran Church in America, she has taught preaching at Yale Divinity School, Princeton Theological Seminary, Hebrew Union College, and in the DMin program of the Association of Chicago Theological Schools. In 2007, she served as president of the Academy of Homiletics. Her numerous writings related to preaching include *Transforming the Stone* and *Marking Time*. This sermon was preached at the Chautauqua United Methodist Renewal Center in Chautauqua, New York, on July 31, 2007.

---

*Isaiah 56:1–8 · Acts 8:26–40*

It had not occurred to Philip to go down from Jerusalem to Gaza. Philip had just completed a very successful preaching mission in Samaria. Response had been heart-warming—more than most preachers ever hope for. Many baptisms, both women and men. Those gathered in Jerusalem were thrilled at the news. But all of this was a bit strange because Philip hadn't been called as a preacher. Remember? He had been set apart as a deacon to care for the widows and orphans. Why was he preaching instead of distributing

Part Three: Calling for Hospitality

food? Who gave Philip the authority to baptize? Peter and John must have worried about such things, for they hurried off to Samaria! They went to pray for the Holy Spirit to come upon those who had been baptized. However, God didn't seem concerned and called Philip on a new mission.

"Then an angel of the Lord said to Philip: 'Get up and go towards the south to the road that goes down from Jerusalem to Gaza.' (This is a wilderness road.)" (Acts 8:26). Or, according to the RSV, "a desert road." It's a little aside directed to the reader. "This is *erene*"—a desert road. Without raising any questions, Philip got up and went.

Now on that same road there was an Ethiopian, a eunuch, a minister of the Candace, queen of the Ethiopians. The narrator slows us down, saying each word with care. A eunuch. An Ethiopian. The very word means swarthy-skinned. Not a native of the area. To Homer, Ethiopia was the farthest known dwelling place of humankind. The place where the sun set. An Ethiopian reading aloud from the scroll of Isaiah. Was he an Ethiopian Jew, one of those called proselytes? How was it that he had his own copy of the scroll of Isaiah? Such things the text doesn't tell us. Only this: he was an Ethiopian. And he was a eunuch.

Five times in the story the narrator repeats the word *eunuch*. We never know his name, but we can't forget that he was a eunuch. A eunuch, commonly defined as a castrated male—though the Bible also includes more metaphorical meanings. He was a male, but not quite a man, often selected to be in charge of a harem—what could be safer? He had been chosen by the queen to oversee her treasury. A very important official. A man who traveled freely from Africa to Jerusalem—not on foot, but in a chariot. He was a powerful man—but he was still a eunuch. "A dry tree" they called him, sometimes behind his back, other times to his face. A dry tree on a desert road. It is clear he is a learned man, reading the scroll of Isaiah. Had he ever read the Holiness Code in the book of Deuteronomy?

"No one whose testicles are crushed or whose penis is cut off shall be admitted to the assembly of the Lord" (Deut 23:1).

The text is clear. It was not up for debate. The eunuch was on his way back home from Jerusalem. Had he gone to Jerusalem to worship in the temple? Did he actually think he would be welcome in the assembly of the Lord?

"Then the Spirit said to Philip, 'Go over to this chariot and join it'" (Acts 8:29). Again, it was not Philip's idea. How could Philip trust the guidance of the Spirit? Earlier in this book of Acts, before Jesus ascended into heaven, he spoke these last words to his disciples before he left the earth: "But you will receive power when the Holy Spirit has come upon you; and you will be my witnesses in Jerusalem, in all Judea and Samaria, and to the ends of the earth" (Acts 1:8). We know Philip had been to Samaria. Now the Spirit is calling him to go to a man who has come to the ends of the earth. It won't be the last time this happens in the book of Acts. The Spirit keeps sending people where they never thought of going.

Philip could hear the eunuch reading aloud from the scroll of the prophet Isaiah. "Do you understand what you are reading?" Philip asked. "How can I, unless someone guides me?" the eunuch answered (Acts 8:30–31). Then he invited Philip to get into the chariot and sit beside him. For many people that would have caused a moment of hesitation—to sit beside a dark-skinned eunuch on what seems to be a deserted desert road. "About whom, may I ask you, does the prophet say this, about himself or about someone else?" (Acts 8:34) Then Philip began to speak . . .

But wait. Have we allowed the eunuch's question to hang in the air? "About whom does the prophet say this, about himself or about someone else?" It's a very good question—and it's almost impossible for us as Christians not to jump in with the answer. We know this is one of the Suffering Servant songs (though Isaiah never called it that). To the eunuch, Isaiah might have meant someone like him. Someone to whom justice had been denied. Someone who felt like a root out of dry ground. "Was the prophet like him?" the eunuch might have wondered. Some of our Jewish sisters and brothers read these words and see their own people, led away like lambs to the slaughter, their life taken away from the earth. "About whom, may I ask you, does the prophet say this, about himself or about someone else?"

Then Philip began to speak, and, starting with Isaiah, he proclaimed to the eunuch the good news about Jesus. But Jesus wasn't in the text. As Christians we believe the Spirit who told Philip to join that chariot revealed Jesus where the name was not written. Or to frame it differently: Isaiah's words had meaning within Isaiah's own time, but when Jesus' followers tried to make sense of his tragic death they "found" Jesus in Isaiah's servant. However we frame it, one thing is clear: without a witness beyond the text, Philip could not have seen Jesus within the text.

I wonder how far they rode together on that desert road? How far did they read in the scroll of Isaiah? Did they unroll the scroll as far as Isa 56?

> Do not let the foreigner joined to the LORD say, "The LORD will surely separate me from his people"; and do not let the eunuch say,

> "I am just a dry tree." For thus says the LORD: to the eunuchs who keep my sabbaths, who choose the things that please me and hold fast my covenant, I will give, in my house and within my walls, a monument and a name better than sons and daughters; I will give them an everlasting name that shall not be cut off. (Isa 56:3–5)

Could it be true? A place within God's household, a name better than sons or daughters for the childless eunuch? An everlasting name that shall not be cut off? It seems likely that the author of Acts saw Isa 56 as the frame for this story. This section of Isaiah is a favorite portion of Scripture for Luke in the Gospel and in this book of Acts. Here, in this one story, we see a man who is both a foreigner and a eunuch.

But how could Isaiah dare to say what he said? Surely he knew the Holiness Code. What authority did he have to set that prohibition aside? That word was written down. "The spirit of the Lord GOD is upon me," wrote Isaiah, "because the LORD has anointed me . . . to bring good news to the oppressed, to bind up the brokenhearted . . ." (Isa 61:1). The Spirit didn't wait until Jesus stood up in the synagogue. The Spirit anointed Isaiah to speak good news of welcome to the eunuch, even though the words written down said it should not be so. Centuries later, the Spirit opened Philip's eyes to see Jesus in the ancient scroll even though the name wasn't written there.

How far would the Spirit take Philip that day on the desert road? How far will the Spirit take us today? Where is the Holy Spirit calling the church in our time? I don't claim that this Acts text is about welcoming gay and lesbian people into the assembly of God—though it's not difficult to find parallels in this story of a man who was defined, at least in part, as a sexual misfit. We're not completely sure what the word *eunuch* means. Of course, New Testament writers hadn't ever heard of the word *homosexual*, but some say the word is there even when it's not!

Our churches have reached an exegetical impasse. Scholars continue to disagree about the exact meaning of texts in Romans and 1 Corinthians. As New Testament scholar Krister Stendahl reminds us, "The Church and the Scriptures live by interpretation, not by repristination. Faithful interpretation is faith-filled creativity."[1] This is how the Bible itself works with texts. Isaiah, writing after the exile, spoke a word of promise to eunuchs that overturned the words written down. Philip heard Jesus' name in Isaiah through a witness beyond the words in the text. The words written down urge us to see more than the words written down.

---

1. Stendahl, "Can Bishops Tell the Truth?," 188.

So it happened, as they went along the road, the eunuch suddenly said, "Look, here is water!" How could it be? The narrator told us at the beginning that this is a desert road. There shouldn't be any water! "Look, here is water!" said the eunuch. "What is to prevent me from being baptized?" (Acts 8:36) "Everything!" we shout: the prohibitions in the Scripture, centuries of tradition, the threat to church unity, the fear in our bones. But here is water, water on a desert road. The eunuch doesn't wait for Philip to answer. He commands his chariot to stop. He believes there is nothing to prevent his being baptized. So both of them go down into the water, the Ethiopian eunuch and Philip, splashing in the scroll of Isaiah.

It could happen in our time. Even in the church. "You will receive power when the Holy Spirit has come upon you," Jesus said. For the words written down urge us to see more than the words written down. Sometimes God makes a river where there isn't one. "Look! Here is water! What is to prevent me from being baptized?" What is to exclude me from the household of God?

# 16

## A Divine Flame

### Deborah A. Appler

The Reverend Dr. Deborah A. Appler, an ordained elder in the United Methodist Church, is the Associate Professor of Old Testament/Hebrew Bible at Moravian Theological Seminary in Bethlehem, Pennsylvania. Before arriving at Moravian, she worked extensively with the United Methodist Publishing House and was also a pastor. This sermon was originally preached in March 2014 to a theologically diverse congregation with a multiplicity of beliefs about what constitutes Christian marriage.

---

*Song of Songs 2:16—3:4; 8:6–7*

Desire.
Longing.
Wanting to be touched, to be held, to be loved and to love—to burn hot with desire for someone we care for with our whole heart and soul.

These feelings are freely expressed through the erotic words dripping like honey from the mouths of the lovers in the biblical book Song of Songs as they boldly sing, "Let him kiss me with the kisses of his mouth! For your love is better than wine" (Song 1:2), or "Let my love come to his garden, let him eat its luscious fruit" (Song 4:16b), where the garden is the metaphor for and place of erotic intimacy. This couple's passion and commitment for each other is further evident through their stolen embraces as they transcend many barriers to find joy in each other's arms.

The love between these two partners burns hot! It consumes them as they seek time together in passion's embrace. The words and images in this biblical song or collection of songs resemble love songs and poetry that we sing today. It is difficult not to feel the same longing and ardor in Peter Gabriel's love song, in which we see the doorway of a thousand churches "in your eyes,"[1] or the passion burning in Martha and the Vandellas "Heat Wave."[2] The popular song by The Bangles from the late 1980s draws us even closer to the Song of Songs, as one lover asks another, "Am I only dreaming, or is this burning an eternal flame?"[3]

Here the singer's claim of ownership of her lover is reminiscent of the mutual commitment of the biblical Song: "I belong to my lover and he belongs to me" (Song 2:16a CEB). The "eternal flame" mirrors the enduring love sung about in the sacred text that assures us that such love is a gift from God: "For love is as strong as death, passionate love unrelenting as the grave. Its darts are darts of fire—divine flame!" (Song 8:6b CEB). These songs celebrate love and longing—the erotic in relationships and the passionate flame that continues to burn when Divine love is present.

Furthermore, they play on the desires, dreams, and sensory pleasures of the erotic in human relationships, as does the Song of Songs. But what do these earthy songs that embarrass us when we read them aloud in church and the love behind them have to do with God? This is the question that was asked when the canon was being finalized. Song of Songs was almost omitted because it was deemed too erotic. Further, the Song celebrates sex for the sake of pleasure and not with a goal of procreating. It isn't even clear that the couple is married. In many ways this sacred song is revolutionary and audacious. Thankfully, Rabbi Akiva intervened: "For all the Writings are holy, but Song of Songs is the Holy of Holies."[4] His words draw us to the holiest part of the temple, where God resides on the mercy seat of the ark. Early Jewish interpreters read this book as an allegory that represented the love between God and the people of Israel, while for Christians it signified

---

1. Peter Gabriel, "In Your Eyes," *So* (Geffen, 1986).
2. Martha and the Vandellas, "Heat Wave," *Heat Wave* (Gordy, 1963).
3. The Bangles, "Eternal Flame," *Everything* (CBS, 1989). I used this song as my call to worship, and it was well received and tied together the themes of my sermon.
4. Mishnah Yadayim 3:5, in Schiffman, *Texts and Traditions*, 120.

the love between Christ and the church. Neither allowed for the possibility that the songs portrayed love between human partners.

However, biblical scholar Renita Weems takes issue with those who wish to ignore the humanness of the eroticism in the Song of Songs. She writes, "The sexual part of our humanity is as strong as death and as unquenchable as fire. That is because sex is frequently the drama around which we attempt desperately to capture our deepest desires, our most feverish longings, our recurrent dreams, and our most aching loneliness."[5] Today's interpreters are willing to approach the Song of Songs as both a celebration of the erotic in our human relationships as well as an allegory for spiritual union with God.

The drama in Song of Songs plays out in eight chapters as two lovers playfully lose and find each other, and search for time and places of intimacy to explore their love. The joy that they receive through the sensual pleasures of taste, smell, touch, voice, and sight is illustrated in the language of nature—graceful animals, seed-filled pomegranates, stags, lilies, and succulent grapes—and is suggestive, to say the least.

The identity of these lovers is somewhat mysterious and elusive. In the text they are two people passionately in love but there appear to be dangers and obstacles in their way. What we do know is that the woman identifies herself as a Shulammite—probably by her geographical origin—while we know little about her partner. Is he a young shepherd or a powerful king?

Further, the lovers are constantly hiding from someone or in search of one another. The woman sings, "I looked for him and I could not find him" (Song 3:1); her partner cries out, "Come back, come back, Shulammite! Come back, come back, so we may admire you" (Song 6:13). Does their constant search for each other illustrate the ups and downs of relationships or do societal forces keep them apart?

There is danger in this relationship. As the woman searches for her lover, she is beaten, stripped, and possibly raped by the sentinels. She laments, "They struck me, bruised me, and took my shawl away from me" (Song 5:7 CEB). Could this violence against her be retribution for the Shulammite's disregard for societal norms as she acts independently, speaks openly about her love, and searches for her lover so boldly in the streets? In a world where relationships are often controlled and arranged by a father or brother, is the Shulammite's conduct unbecoming? Perhaps this woman's family has already promised her to another partner and she defies her

---

5. Weems, *What Matters Most*, 4.

gendered place in society by holding tight to the one whom her soul loves. Is this couple's love doomed like Romeo and Juliet, Lancelot and Guinevere, and Ennis Del Mar and Jack Twist in *Brokeback Mountain*?

Or perhaps this couple is endangered because they choose to ignore class distinctions. In the sixth verse of chapter 1, the woman attributes her dark skin color to being forced by her brothers to work in the fields. She exclaims, "Don't stare at me because I'm darkened by the sun's gaze" (Song 1:6 CEB). Does the kingly procession celebrated in 3:6–11 suggest that the Shulammite and maybe even King Solomon might have entered into an unequal economic relationship without society's approval?

Or could they be harassed because they are involved in a unsanctioned interracial or interethnic relationship? The woman boldly proclaims herself to be "black and beautiful," like the black tents of the Kedar nomads (Song 1:5). Is she one of Solomon's foreign wives from Cush or from other parts of the world? While there appears to be societal resistance to these young lovers, it is clear that the woman wants the relationship out in the open as she describes her love's beauty and openly proclaims to her group of friends, "This is my love, this my dearest, daughters of Jerusalem!" (Song 5:16). While some may hope to douse their passion, the flames of desire burn deeply in the hearts of these two lovers.

Christopher King and other scholars have noted that the relationship recounted in the Song of Songs is "transgressive"—that it resists the constricting societal norms as defined by the ancient culture in which these texts were created: a society in which relationships were often based not on the flames of desire but on family needs and tradition—to keep land and property in the household and to maintain the ethnic identity.[6] Today many of these relational barriers in parts of the world have been transcended. Most contemporary churches in the U.S. recognize that the Divine flame of love can burn in the hearts of couples of differing races, ethnicities, and economic backgrounds. Yet there are still men and women in relationships burning deeply with the Divine flame of God who love dangerously and without the support of the church. Some of these couples have experienced violence and censure and attempts to drown the flame, much like the resistance met by the woman in the Song when accosted by the sentinels in the

---

6. Christopher King's "A Love as Fierce as Death: Reclaiming the Song of Songs for Queer Lovers" has been incredibly helpful for thinking through Song of Songs for this sermon, as well as Renita Weems' "Song of Songs" class, taught at Vanderbilt Divinity School in 1994, and her readings of this book.

city. How might the Song's resistance to societal norms and celebration of love play out in our churches and culture today?

The Song of Songs cries out to us to break down the religious and societal barriers that privilege heterosexual love over same-sex relationships. This sacred text celebrates the flame of love that is God-given to gay and straight couples alike. And furthermore, it's not as if same-sex lovers any more than heterosexual lovers set out to break down social barriers. They fall in love. King reminds us that who we love and commit ourselves to is not determined by "lifestyle choices" or sexual preferences![7] Our relationships are cemented by the passionate and unrelenting love described in 8:6—the result of the Divine flame—the darts of fire that securely attach two hearts together in love, regardless of gender or sexuality. These flames of God have a tendency to strike in many wonderful and uncontrollable ways.

The flame that burns in the lovers' hearts is more than fleeting passion or intense feeling. King reminds us that the Song of Songs focuses on an "ethic of intimacy."[8] While the Shulammite and her lover and other loving couples might not have the blessing of many ecclesial bodies or parts of society, the Song recognizes that the couple's love is ordained by God—a higher power—and is held securely in place by the seal over the heart and the signet on the arm and a Divine flame: "I belong to my lover and he belongs to me" (Song 2:16).

The erotic in the Song of Songs experienced through all of the senses—pleasure through touch, smell, sound, taste, sight—offers us insight into the Divine. The Divine flames of love that ignite an unquenchable mutual passion in the hearts of same-sex and heterosexual lovers is not only a gift from the Holy but also a portal into understanding more fully our relationships with each other and with God. The mystics knew this, as did Rabbi Akiva, who fought to make sacred this Holy book. The erotic and the Divine are closely intertwined. As theologian Carter Heyward writes,

> The erotic is our most fully embodied experience of the love of God. As such, it is the source of our capacity for transcendence, the "crossing over" among ourselves, making connections between ourselves in relation. The erotic is the divine Spirit's yearning,

---

7. King, "Love as Fierce as Death," 130.
8. Ibid., 126.

through our bodyselves, toward mutually empowering relation, which is our most fully embodied experience of God as love.[9]

God calls all humans to a passionate relationship with the Holy that is often more fully understood through our human relationships. Even when our faith communities and society, those modern-day sentinels, refuse to bless the love that God has created and ordained, and try to douse the flames with water, they can't, "for love is as strong as death, passionate love unrelenting as the grave. Its darts are darts of fire—divine flame!" (Song 8:6b).

Desire.

Longing.

Wanting to be touched, to be held, to be loved and to love—to burn hot with desire for someone we care for with our whole heart and soul.

May the fires of God, the Divine flame, ignite and bring unimaginable passion and joy in each and every one of our relationships—a delectable taste of the Divine. So be it. Amen.

---

9. Heyward, *Touching Our Strength*, 99.

# 17

## Luke's Stonewall

### Mona West

The Reverend Dr. Mona West is the Director of the Office of Formation and Leadership Development for the Metropolitan Community Churches. Originally ordained in the Southern Baptist denomination in 1987, she transferred her ordination credentials to the MCC in 1992. She holds a PhD in Old Testament Studies and has taught in several colleges and universities, as well as serving as a pastor at Cathedral of Hope in Dallas, Texas. She is the author of numerous publications and coeditor of *Take Back the Word: A Queer Reading of the Bible*. This sermon was preached at Church of the Trinity MCC in Sarasota, Florida, on Father's Day, 2007.

---

*Luke 7:36–50*

Happy Father's Day to you all! I don't know about you, but I love to research holidays and religious observances. You never know when the information you find could help you win a game of *Trivial Pursuit* or help you get on *Jeopardy!*

Did you know that Father's Day began in America in 1909? Sonora Smart got the idea of setting aside a special day to honor her father, William Smart, while she was listening to a Mother's Day sermon. William became widowed when his wife died while giving birth to their sixth child. William raised all six children by himself. When Sonora thought of a date to honor her father she decided his birthday would be a fitting occasion, so on June 19, 1910, the first unofficial Father's Day celebration was held.

Later, in 1924, President Calvin Coolidge supported the idea of a national Father's Day, and by 1956 a joint resolution of Congress recognized Father's Day as a national observance. In 1966 Lyndon Johnson declared the third Sunday of June as Father's Day, and in 1972 Richard Nixon signed the date into law.

There have been lots of wonderful articles this week suggesting ways to celebrate Father's Day, particularly what kind of gift to give Dad. (Of course, the number one gift is still a barbeque grill.)

And we do give thanks for all those in our congregation and in our lives who are fathers, grandfathers, godfathers, or who have been like fathers to us. I hope you will find some special way today to communicate your love and appreciation to these folks.

*But I also want to point out that for many of us, days like Father's Day and Mother's Day can bring up mixed feelings.*

Not all of us have good relationships with our fathers or mothers, sons or daughters. So on days like today, whatever tension might exist in those relationships can be heightened. Days like today can also cause grief to well up in some of us who have lost a parent or a child.

These issues can be especially complicated if there is pain and rejection over one's sexual orientation or gender identity. So, when we offer our prayers of thanksgiving for fathers today, let's also offer prayers of healing for those who are hurting and estranged from their fathers, or perhaps from their mothers and families as well.

I came across a beautiful article by Michael Bronski, a gay activist, who reflected on what it meant to love and honor his father on Father's Day—a day that often coincides with gay pride celebrations in the month of June. Bronski points out that Pride Day is often celebrated on the Sunday closest to the anniversary of the Stonewall uprisings, which took place in New York City on June 28–29, 1969, after police raided a well-known gay bar, the Stonewall Inn. The patrons of the bar were used to police raids, but on that night there was a group that had had enough. They were drag queens and they refused "to go quietly into that good night." Their resistance sparked civil rights demonstrations throughout the gay community, and many believe their actions gave birth to the modern gay liberation movement. Bronski muses,

## Part Three: Calling for Hospitality

> This tension between Gay Pride and Father's Day isn't just a scheduling conflict. It is—for many gay men—a time to reflect upon the extraordinarily complicated position of being a gay man who has a heterosexual father.... It is precisely this exaggerated cumbersomeness, this emotionally fragile distance—between father and son, straight and gay, between generations, between dreams and reality—that make gay men and their fathers a prism for viewing all our challenges of parenthood and childhood, even on this day of celebrating them.[1]

The writer of Luke's Gospel could have been part of the Stonewall revolution. I don't think Luke was a drag queen, but Luke's Gospel more than any other in the New Testament features the marginalized and outcasts of society as major actors in God's work of liberation.

For Luke, salvation was not about some future realm of God but the real flesh-and-blood needs of people on earth. It is in Luke's Gospel that Jesus stands up in his hometown synagogue and proclaims, "The Spirit of the Lord is upon me, because [God] has anointed me to bring good news to the poor . . . to proclaim release to the captives and recovery of sight to the blind, to let the oppressed go free, to proclaim the year of the Lord's favor" (4:18–19).

Luke's Stonewall is about the liberating power of the gospel and the way God's love can transform lives—especially the lives of those on the margins. Our story today from Scripture reads like a mini-Stonewall. Just as the drag queens of New York were "women of the city" who brought about liberation through their radical action, this unnamed "woman of the city" in Luke 7 brings about liberation through her radical acts of hospitality.

It is not unusual to find Jesus dining at the house of a Pharisee. He actually has a lot in common with them—they love and respect the law, and so does Jesus; they are devout Jews, and so is Jesus. Jesus' conflict with the Pharisees was about the *abuse* of religion and the law. (We also have no indication that Simon the Pharisee had invited Jesus to dinner to trap him in some kind of theological or political argument.)

What is at issue in this story is hospitality—the lack of it from the most obvious of places, and the offer of it from the least likely of places. There were three customary signs of hospitality offered to guests in the ancient Near East: washing their dusty feet, refreshing them with a bit of oil on their heads, and welcoming them with a kiss of peace. Simon the

---

1. Bronski, "The Bridge to Manhood."

Pharisee had done none of these, yet he criticizes the unnamed woman for doing so. Why?

We are told she is a "woman of the city," a "sinner." More than likely she was poor and forced into prostitution in order to survive. And she crashes the dinner party!

There is something about Jesus that compels her to come to the dinner party uninvited. There is something about Jesus that compels her to offer a hospitality that breaks through the barriers of hostility and judgment that would keep her out. She is so overcome with her experience of Jesus that she weeps. Her tears wash Jesus' feet and she dries them with her hair. She had brought an alabaster jar of ointment to anoint Jesus' feet, and she never stops kissing his feet while she anoints them. What an extravagant and radical offer of hospitality!

And Simon—who as host has offered nothing—becomes judgmental. He says to himself, "If this man were a prophet, he would have known who and what kind of woman this is touching him" (7:39).

Do you know people like this? People like the woman, whose experiences on the margins of life cause them to recognize the love of God in Christ Jesus? Their response to that love is a radical and extravagant hospitality that welcomes not only God into their lives, but others who are on this same human journey.

Or people like Simon, whose attitudes about who is and is not acceptable to God cause him to withhold basic hospitality, cause him to fail to recognize the love of God in his very own house?

The woman's Stonewall—her radical actions—created a space for liberation to occur. In her offer of hospitality she received the extravagant welcome of the living God. Jesus says to her, "Your faith has saved you; go in peace" (7:50).

What do Father's Day, Stonewall, and this story in Luke's Gospel have in common? An invitation. An invitation to offer radical acts of love and hospitality in an effort to overcome barriers that separate. Radical acts of love and hospitality that overcome judgment and criticism, that might even have the power to heal, renew, and transform our world. Which includes our fathers and mothers, and perhaps ourselves as well.

When we experience radical acts of love and hospitality, we too just might hear Jesus' words: "Go in peace."

# 18

## Healing Our -isms

### Irene Monroe

The Reverend Irene Monroe is a *Huffington Post* blogger and a syndicated religion columnist. She holds degrees from Wellesley College and Union Theological Seminary at Columbia University and served as a pastor at an African American church before pursuing her doctoral work as a Ford Fellow at Harvard Divinity School. Her columns appear in twenty-three cities across the U.S., the U.K., and Canada, with a focus on the role fundamentalist religion plays in discrimination against lesbian, gay, bisexual, transgender, and queer people, as well as how religious intolerance and fundamentalism aid in perpetuating other forms of oppression such as racism, sexism, classism, and anti-Semitism. This sermon was originally preached in the historic Riverside Church in New York City for their Pride service on June 27, 2010.

---

*Ephesians 2:11–22*

I come this morning to talk with you about our shared history. Our history of the ongoing struggle for human acceptance at difficult points along the human timeline.

There is an old African legend about the people of Sumer who, once upon a time, struggled for their freedom. And once they obtained it, they never took the time to reflect on their freedom and the people who had been left behind because of the struggle.

"What became of the black people of Sumer?" a traveler asked the old man. "For the ancient records show that the people of Sumer were black. What happened to them?"

"Ah," the old man sighed. "They lost their history, so they died..."

On this Pride Sunday, as we celebrate this festive moment together, we must not forget our courageous lesbian, gay, bisexual, and transgender foresisters and forebrothers who have paved the way for us to be here today. Their early struggles to be visible make our visibility that much more sacred and profound. Our visibility is the fruit of their early struggles and their defiant faith in the face of opposition, which is why remembering the past allows us to better celebrate the present. And this history we must not forget.

Although Christians do not necessarily make the connection, if we all knew our history we would know that lesbian, gay, bisexual, and transgender people stand firmly on the shoulders of the early Christians. Until the fourth century, when the Roman emperor Constantine converted to Christianity, Christians were despised as much as lesbian, gay, bisexual, and transgender people are today. As a matter of fact, to be called a Christian was considered a religious epithet. It subjected Christians to ridicule, hate crimes, and Christian-bashing in much the same way that we lesbian, gay, bisexual, and transgender people continue to experience today.

In 1998, Matthew Shepard, a twenty-one-year-old first-year student at the University of Wyoming, was bludgeoned and then nailed to a wooden fence, like a hunting trophy, all because he was gay. Likewise, in 35 CE, Stephen, a follower of Jesus, was stoned to death because he was a Christian, becoming the first Christian martyr on record. (The Apostle Paul, before he saw the risen Christ on the road to Damascus and stopped his Christian-bashing, was one of the many approving bystanders at Stephen's stoning.)

Just as lesbian, gay, bisexual, and transgender people transformed the pejorative term *queer* into a positive word of self-reference, Christians transformed the word *Christian* into one of self-reverence.

Having known this history, I found calling myself a queer Christian neither blasphemous nor oxymoronic. For both are tied to the ongoing struggle for human acceptance, just at different points along the human timeline.

# Part Three: Calling for Hospitality

When you think about it, religion has become a peculiar institution in the theater of human life. The Latin root *religio* means "to bind, tie, or fasten together," yet much of the binding religion has done has been binding people's shared hatred. Religion has played a salient role in discrimination against all people at different times throughout history, including in this country.

For example, I come out of a black religious tradition born of struggle for human acceptance. When slave masters gave my ancestors the Bible, their intent was not to make us better Christians, but instead better slaves. The Bible, at least according to the slave masters, provided the legitimate biblical sanction for American slavery.

However, my ancestors turned this authoritative text—which was meant to aid them in acclimating to their life of servitude—into an incendiary text that not only ignited slave revolts and abolitionists movements but also the nation's civil rights movement. The Bible told us African Americans how to do what must be done. And so Nat Turner revolted against slavery, and Harriet Tubman conducted a railroad out of it. My ancestors expanded not only the understanding of what it meant to be human but also the parameters of what it meant to be a Christian.

Knowing this history, I find that calling myself a queer African American Christian makes me neither less black nor less Christian. For it is all tied to the ongoing struggle for human acceptance, just at different points along the human timeline.

Our text this morning talks about the ongoing struggle for human acceptance at a difficult point along the human timeline. The Ephesians were people of various backgrounds and nationalities. The two largest and conflicting ethnic groups in Ephesus were the Jews and Gentiles. The temple the Jews and Gentiles attended was a divided place of worship. Only Jews could enter the inner court of the temple; Gentile visitors were relegated to the outer court.

The wall of partition in the temple symbolized the temple's system of ecclesiastical segregation. When Paul writes, "[Christ] abolished the law with its commandments and ordinances, that he might create in himself one new humanity in place of the two, thus making peace" (Eph 2:15), he is referring to Christ's lifting of the legal restrictions that maintained a system of segregation, that perpetuated a state of hostility between the Jews and Gentiles. When Paul later tells the Gentiles, "You are no longer strangers and aliens, but you are citizens with the saints and also members of the household of God" (2:19), the Gentiles no longer had temporary or limited rights in the community. Gentiles were now allowed every privilege and status formerly denied them, for they were accepted into the family of God. There were no longer insiders and outsiders; there was no more a system of separate but equal. The belief was that anyone may come into this temple, since no one group of people is better than another. I'm reminded of Paul's letter to the Galatians, when he writes that in Christ Jesus "there is no longer Jew or Greek . . . slave or free . . . male or female" (Gal 3:28), which also means for us today there is no longer straight or gay, for we are all one in Christ Jesus. In breaking down the wall of partition that existed in the temple, Paul not only broke down the hostility between the Jews and Gentiles but also reconciled both groups to God as one body.

Of course, even though the gospel breaks down these walls of partition, the church continues to erect them all these years later.

Richard Allen, for example, encountered many walls of partition in his life. Born in 1760 in Philadelphia, the slave of a Quaker master, he became a free black man and in the 1780s converted to Methodism, becoming an itinerant Methodist preacher. One of the walls of partition that he could not tear down in the all-white St. George's Methodist Church was racism. So in 1797, Richard Allen founded Mother Bethel African Methodist Church, the first black Methodist Church in Philadelphia, and in 1816 he led African Methodists into a separate denomination after many years of struggle against white control. The African Methodist Episcopal Church is now the oldest black denomination in this country.

Another wall of partition that has been erected has to do with the role of women in the church. When Christians turn to the edict in 1 Timothy that women should not be permitted "to teach or to have authority over a man" but should "keep silent" (1 Tim 2:12), too often the result is that women encounter the partition of sexism.

And most major denominations in this country still maintain their walls of partition when it comes to the acceptance and spiritual needs of lesbian, gay, bisexual, and transgender people.

So, what might be the wall of partition that is erected here at Riverside Church? What might be your form of institutionalized segregation disguised or misunderstood as the teachings of Christ?

One wall of partition within LGBTQ communities is the ongoing infighting. I say this because race, unfortunately, continues to be one of the fault lines in many of our Pride festivals across the country, as does gender identity.

## Part Three: Calling for Hospitality

Long before Black and Latino Prides marched to their soulful and salsa beats in the late 1980s and early 1990s, respectively, Lesbian Pride marches came on the scene in the 1970s. And they were protest marches publicly denouncing, at the time, the political stronghold and exclusionary practices of Gay Pride events—as Wikipedia correctly noted—"by white gay men at the expense of lesbians in general and women of color in particular." By the 1990s, Dyke Marches emerged.

We may have forgotten this history in our LGBTQ movement—a history that represents the affirmation of a certain defiant faith in the face of opposition, which marks another difficult point along the human timeline.

It is not enough just to look outside ourselves to see the places where society is broken. It is not enough to talk about institutions, churches, and workplaces that fracture and separate people based on race, religion, gender, and sexual orientation. We must also look at the ways we as the LGBTQ community can be both the oppressed and the oppressor. We must look at the ways that we ourselves can manifest these bigotries. We cannot heal the world if we have not healed ourselves. So perhaps the greatest task, and the most difficult work we must first do, is to heal ourselves. And this work must be done in relationship with our justice work in the world.

But we're not alone.

New York ought to be ashamed of itself when it comes to our right to marry. If New York understood its history, in terms of our contributions, it would understand that without us there would be no Broadway, no fashion industry, no style, no church music, just to name a few examples. We need New York to get with the program and pass its marriage equality bill![1]

To me, democracy is an ongoing process where people are part of a participatory government working to dismantle all existing discriminatory laws that truncate their full participation in society. The work of democracy is rooted in justice and social change, allowing us—along this troubling human timeline—to see the faces and hear the voices in our society that are damned, disinherited, disrespected, and dispossessed. Democracy can only begin to work when those relegated to the fringes of society can begin to sample what those in the mainstream take for granted as their inalienable rights.

African American cultural critic bell hooks states that she begins her analysis at the margin because it is a space of radical openness, and it gives

---

1. New York legalized same-gender marriage in 2011, almost a year to the day that this sermon was preached.

one an oppositional gaze from which to see the world, unknown to the oppressor. It is at the margin where you can see injustice being done. It is not only a site where you can honestly critique the oppressive structures in society that keep us wounded as a people, but it is also a site that can heal us as a people—both the oppressed and the oppressor.[2]

In *The Old Man and the Sea*, Ernest Hemingway said that the world breaks us all, but some of us grow strong in those broken places. Martin Luther King Jr.'s teachings invite us to grow strong in our broken places—not only to mend the sin-sick world in which we live, but also to mend the sin-sick world that we carry around within us. And we can only do that if we are willing to look both inward and outward, healing ourselves of the bigotry, biases, and demons that chip away at our efforts to work toward justice and diversity in our own community.

For instance, I know that the struggle against racism is only legitimate if I am also fighting anti-Semitism, homophobia, sexism, and classism—not only out in the world but also in myself. Otherwise, I am creating an ongoing cycle of abuse that goes on, unexamined and unaccounted for.

People change in the course of their lives, and when they change for the better it's because they have torn down a wall of partition they were once holding up. The Apostle Paul changed in the course of his life. When Paul tore down his wall of bigotry, he was then able to build up his ministry.

Paul's letter to the Ephesians emphasizes the inclusivity of the church as the body of Christ. Sometimes the walls of hostility that we've erected in our community have made us foreigners and strangers among one another. And these walls will remain erect until we cure ourselves of our fears and hatred of one another. Pride is about the varied expressions of the life, gifts, and talents of the entire LGBTQ community. But the divisions in our community during Pride also show us something troubling and broken within ourselves, which the gospel comes to heal.

As LGBTQ people, we fail to realize that our gift and our struggle is related to being a diverse community within ourselves, and our diversity should not dilute our commitment to and love for one another; rather, our diversity should teach us more about the gift of complexity, and by extension teach the larger society.

The Kwanzaa principle of Umoja—unity—must take root in our self-understanding of who we are and what we decide to be as both a people and a community. In understanding the interconnectedness between

---

2. See bell hooks, *Feminist Theory: From Margin to Center*.

individuals and community, African historian John Mbiti famously said, "I am, because we are; and since we are, therefore I am."[3]

In the face of our own self-respect and in embracing the Kwanzaa principle of Umoja:

The fighting among us must stop!

The distrust among us must stop!

The competitiveness among us must stop!

We must cure ourselves of our indifference to each other's oppressions, whether related to class, gender, race, religion, sexual orientation, gender identity, or whatever it might be. As a community we must all pitch in. The belief among us that one oppression is greater than another oppression sets up a hierarchy of oppressions and keeps us fighting. The moral and spiritual challenge before us is that united we can stand as a community, or divided we can fall.

"I am, because we are; and since we are, therefore I am."

---

3. Mbiti, *African Religions and Philosophy*, 141.

# 19

## The Storm Is Passing Over

### Mary Foulke

The Reverend Mary Foulke is the Rector of St. Mary's Episcopal Church, Manhattanville, in New York City. She previously served as Senior Associate Minister at St. Luke in the Fields Episcopal Church in New York City, as well as the Chaplain at St. Luke's School. This sermon was preached in the historic Riverside Church in New York City on Pride Sunday, June 24, 2012.

---

*1 Samuel 17 · Mark 4:35–41*

"The storm is passing over. The storm is passing over. The storm is passing over, hallelujah!"[1] At first glance (first listen) this song seems to be sung from the other side, from a place of hope where the calm is somehow visible. An end is in sight.

It is not the song the disciples sing as the boat is tossed and the lighting is flashing around them, they can only see the storm, and they panic.

Let us start at the beginning.

Jesus said to the disciples, "Let us go across to the other side" (Mark 4:35). This is Jesus' call: let us go ... across ... to the other side. It is not a journey of "Let's take the safest route," nor is it a journey of "Let's sleep on it

---

1. Reverend Foulke opens her sermon by recalling the hymn "The Storm Is Passing Over," written by Charles A. Tindley.

and start fresh in the morning." The journey with Jesus is one of right now, crossing over, venturing to a new place, seeking out the other. The journey with Jesus is one of change, and change is always a bit stormy . . . or worse.

Charles Albert Tindley, who wrote the lyrics and music to "The Storm Is Passing Over," was a man who crossed over to the other side. He died in 1933, and his whole life was a journey of change. Tindley was born to a free woman, Esther Miller Tindley, in 1851; his father, Charles Tindley, was enslaved. Of course his parents wouldn't have been legally married, though according to most accounts their relationship was recognized by their community as a marriage. Unfortunately, Esther did not live to see Charles Albert's father freed or to gain legal status as his wife; she died in 1855. Charles Albert was raised by Caroline, his sister—or his aunt, depending upon the source you read. He was raised among slaves near Berlin, Maryland, and never formally educated.

Charles Albert Tindley crossed over from the world of slavery to emancipation and the beginning of freedom. We could argue whether it was by birth or by history, by faith or by education (he found tutors and friends to teach him, including learning Hebrew at a synagogue in Philadelphia); and he was ordained a Methodist minister in 1889. As the story goes, the church where he had once worked as a janitor for no money became the church to which he returned as a pastor, a church that grew under his leadership from 130 to ten thousand people—crossing over from servitude to leadership.

The disciples were in the boat, but I think they were not quite ready to cross over. They certainly were not ready for the weather. Isn't it that way for us? I mean, getting in the boat with Jesus seemed like a good idea at the time, when the sun was shining, but . . .

Of course liberal Christians want to get in the boat with, to be inclusive of, lesbian, gay, bisexual, transgender, and questioning people . . . But some even in the liberal church might ask, do they have to express themselves all the time? Do they have to get married? Isn't it their fault that we have to talk about sex in church?

Today I am telling you—gay people are not the storm. LGBTQ people are not the storm. We might be caught up in the breezes on the outside, but let me tell you what the storm really is. The storm is all of our deep and abiding shame about sexuality in general; the storm is all of our hatred of our own bodies; the storm is the soul-twisting sickness of our culture that allows horrific abuse of children to go without comment because we are too ashamed to see it or to stop it. That is the storm.

It is painful to acknowledge. A wound that has not healed because it has been covered up. I bring it up today because we cannot address why LGBTQ pride is a gift, a blessing for all people, a path to healing for many communities, unless we first acknowledge and honor the brokenness and violence that is all around us. Sexual violence and all its attendant forces—sexism, heterosexism, racism, phobias, and hatreds—are the giant Goliath. We see the devastation in the Sandusky child sex abuse trial, or in the prevalence of sex trafficking in our own city and nation as well as abroad. The illnesses of eating disorders of all kinds, depressions, and addictions are related. You would think that the powers that be would issue a rallying cry to address this deep and pervasive societal problem—that at least insurance companies would want to stop the hemorrhage of money that goes to treating the damage. But the powers are afraid, as Saul was afraid. It's too big, too scary.

But thank God there are Davids. Davids who speak out about their own experiences, who speak up for those who cannot speak for themselves, who are not so much warriors (at least not yet) as they are shepherds. Protectors. These shepherds have the smooth stones of making connections, of understanding that the pain of one hurts many, of knowing that they are not alone. These shepherds, no matter how young or untrained, will slay the giant. The idea that David did not have to be fully prepared, did not have to be of a certain age or status in order to engage the threat, is powerful.

We don't have to wait until we've worked out our personal issues, or until our children are grown, or until the degree is completed, or until we've received tenure, or until we're off public assistance, or until we've gotten the promotion, or whatever. We are called by Jesus to cross over, to get in the boat now and set sail for justice and freedom and love.

Last year at this time I proposed to my partner of then twenty-three years; we were married by a community of friends on the beach in 1991. This time the state of New York was climbing in the boat with us. I was not so sure, but however uncomfortable I was, I knew I wanted to cross to the other side. So, last October we celebrated the state of New York's legal recognition of our marriage; it was the twentieth anniversary of our first vows.

The storm of violence still threatens. We can count on the giant, the storm, whatever we call it, to evoke tension, conflict, or even war within and among us. Think of Shakespeare's play *The Tempest*, when a storm conjured the energy of elemental spirits, spent fury, and order overthrown. Even rights that have been gained are contested: employment, housing, marriage, and of course there is no federal protection for any of these.

The nineteenth-century British artist J. M. W. Turner asked sailors to tie him to the mast of a sailing vessel so that he might observe a snowstorm at sea; it was an ordeal that lasted at least four hours and resulted in striking paintings of a boat tossed while on the sea. At my parish at St. Luke in the Fields, we tie ourselves to the mast on Saturday nights as we open our doors to youth ages thirteen to twenty-one who identify as lesbian, gay, bisexual, transgender, queer, questioning, and allies. We see youth who have been kicked out of or have run away from home because of who they are; many have experienced some kind of trauma, a number struggle with mental illness, approximately 30 percent are homeless. We offer a hot meal and a place to stay that is safe. It is a shepherd ministry: we invite connections, we express understanding, and we remind them that they are not alone. Last week, in spite of the many Pride activities, we still had sixty-three youth come to the program. Before June our numbers were closer to ninety. For these kids on the margins, the growing acceptance of LGBTQ persons remains a distant shore. They are often rejected by family and school; if there is a faith community, it is rarely helpful.

Residents of the West Village are frustrated by noisy gatherings of young people. And the young people are certainly in the target group for those disproportionately stopped and frisked—or worse—by the NYPD. A more middle-aged, economically secure, mostly white LGBTQ community who dominate the public perception of what it means to be gay are in danger of thinking themselves (ourselves?) "normal" and thinking these kids are not. But we can do better.

Nothing is too big, no giant is so formidable, no storm of violence so great that we, like David, should not call upon the name of our God. This is what we do today when we march, this is the source of our Pride. In the name of our God, who does not come with sword and spear to harm, but who saves us from the lion and bear; in the name of our God we can rest, knowing that every aspect of our lives—our bodies, our minds, our spirits, our deepest shames and most powerful desires—is precious, beloved, embraced with all tenderness and passion by our Creator. When we stand up as lesbian, gay, bisexual, transgender, questioning people and allies, when we stand with those who are beaten, rejected, and even killed for who we are and what we do with our bodies, we claim the blessing that God has given us in our birth, and the promise that Jesus calls us to live into: we are not alone, we are created for love and community. And we need to stand up to anyone who suggests otherwise. We have gotten in the boat and we are crossing over to the other side. Our message of Pride is not "we're just like everyone else." The message of Pride is "we are different and we praise God for it"—"Peace! Be still!" (Luke 4:39).

The storm is passing over. The transformative power of this song is precisely that it is sung from the middle of the storm, before we see the morning light. It is a song of hope in the present that comes from a deep faith in change, faith that "tho the night is dark, it won't be very long." No storm lasts forever: not slavery, not heterosexism, not even racism and sexism and transphobia. We haven't reached the distant shining shore, but we have this journey with one another. We have courage that comes from making connections, with crossing to the other side, with celebrating—not silencing—our differences. It is a song that Jesus might sing.

Today we celebrate our differences and we proclaim our vulnerability as lesbian, gay, bisexual, transgender, and questioning persons in a sex-obsessed and intimacy-phobic culture. We get in the boat with those LGBTQ teenagers and those on the margins, different from ourselves in some ways—except in our need for love. We march, we dance, we organize, we stand in silent prayer, we shout and sing, "The storm is passing over, hallelujah!"

*Part Four*

Calling for Transformation

# 20

# A Queer Eye for the Straight Bible Reader

MIGUEL A. DE LA TORRE

The Reverend Dr. Miguel A. De La Torre is a highly sought-after speaker, teacher, scholar, and writer who is currently the Professor of Social Ethics and Latino/a Studies at Iliff School of Theology in Denver, Colorado. He is an ordained Baptist minister and has served as the President of the Society of Christian Ethics. He is the author or editor of more than twenty-nine books, including *Doing Christian Ethics from the Margins* and *Liberation Theologies for Arm Chair Theologians*. This sermon is based on a revision of one of his earlier works, titled "Testimonies from Sodom and Gomorrah," which appeared in his commentary on Genesis in the series Belief: A Theological Commentary on the Bible.

---

*Genesis 19:1–11*

Tommy (not his real name) was a good friend. We met in the 1980s at our local Southern Baptist church, where I served as deacon and Sunday school teacher. We were both young, single, "good-looking," and took our faith seriously. We were also "backsliding" Baptists, which meant we enjoyed an occasional glass of wine. Every so often we would invite fellow congregants to join us for a night of fellowship, conversation, music, and, of course, dancing. One night, Tommy stopped by my house for a talk. Considering

PART FOUR: CALLING FOR TRANSFORMATION

our youth, it should not be surprising that our conversation eventually led to the topic of sex. I shared my many sexual temptations. At this point Tommy shared that he too struggled with sexual temptation; however, for him, the temptation was for other males. Tommy, to my shock and horror, was gay. How can a Christian, let alone a Southern Baptist, be a homosexual? I reminded him that homosexuality was a sin, an abomination before God, and a free choice he was making that was morally indefensible.

How did I know this? Because my church told me.

I became a "born again" Christian in my early twenties when I walked down the aisle and gave my heart to Jesus. The church I joined was a loving congregation. People accepted me as family. These loving, gentle people taught me about God, the Bible, and what it meant to be a Christian. Of the many lessons, one was that homosexuality was a sin. Why would I have doubted sincere, faithful Christians whom I admired? They wouldn't lead me astray, right? They pointed to the chapters and verses that showed God's anger toward gays. Converting to Christianity taught me the proper response was to hate homosexuality while still loving the sinner. If I wanted to make this church my home, I had to make sure that my actions toward gays were consistent with what my church said God's view was toward homosexuals—a kinder, gentler form of gay-bashing.

So here I was with my dear friend Tommy. We had become close friends, so shunning him was no longer an option. How could I hate the sin while loving the sinner? I asked Tommy if he wanted to break free from the bondage of sin. He said yes. I asked him if he repented from his sins, took Jesus as his personal Lord and Savior, and believed that through the power of prayer he could become a new creature in Christ. With tears in his eyes he said yes. I asked him if he wanted to be a heterosexual. "Dear God Almighty, yes," he burst out before emotionally breaking down. Tommy, I felt, was well on the road to healing and salvation.

I agreed to be his spiritual partner in the struggle against the evils of homosexuality. We prayed together. We fasted. We cast out the demon of homosexuality. If anyone ever truly wanted to be a heterosexual, if anyone ever truly wanted to stop finding men attractive, if anyone ever truly humbled himself before God to faithfully live a Christian life, it was Tommy. Years went by, and you know what, Tommy was still gay. Tommy did not change, but I did. In a very real sense, Tommy taught me something important about God. For you see, either God is impotent in saving a willing believer from her or his sins, or maybe, just maybe, I have been taught to read the Bible through the eyes of oppressors, no matter how loving and sincere these oppressors appeared. The folks at my church were really nice people, God-fearing and decent; nevertheless, the way they understood their faith oppressed and dishonored our queer brothers and sisters, who, like the rest of us, are created in the very image of God.

The sin that I had to wrestle with was not Tommy's homosexuality but my heterocentricism. It is not homosexuality that displeases God; it is my imposing my sexual orientation on everyone else that is the true abomination. Heterosexual experience has, for the past two thousand years, been affirmed by the church, making it the normative behavior for all of humanity. This patriarchal understanding of sexuality was justified and legitimized by the kind of Christian faith with which I was most familiar. This understanding, however, imposes multiple oppressive structures, not just on the LGBTQ community but also on women, children, and people of color. I began to recognize that if I wanted to move beyond such oppressive structures I would need to adopt a liberationist reading of Scripture—an approach that seeks to understand sexuality from the perspective of those who have been oppressed by how sexuality has historically been defined by Christianity.

For most of my life I had read the Bible through a heterosexual lens that normalizes and legitimizes the imposition of heterosexual patriarchal structures. What I needed was a queer eye for the straight Bible reader. To that end, I returned to one of the most cited Scriptures used to justify the oppression of the LGBTQ community: Genesis 19. As I reflect back on my complicity with heterosexism, it is important to note that because of my orientation, I could not then—and cannot now—speak for the queer community, nor can I provide them with the necessary pedagogy to achieve liberation. To do so would be paternalistic. But to remain silent in the face of oppressive structures because "homosexuality is not my issue" would make me complicit with social structures designed to protect and advance my heterosexual privilege within society, similar to the way white privilege benefits Euro-Americans regardless of their support for or rejection of white supremacy. The only thing that I, as a heterosexual, can say with any integrity concerning LGBTQ issues is how I benefit and am privileged by my heterosexual orientation.

With that said, allow me to begin with the recognition that Sodom's sin is an abomination before God—a perverse and prevalent sin that undermines our nation. It is a lifestyle practiced among the highest echelons of government. Almost all who ever served as U.S. president, in the U.S. Congress, or on the Supreme Court have been guilty of the sin of Sodom. Many of today's religious leaders, specifically those we frequently find on our television screens pleading for contributions, have also engaged in the lifestyle marked by Sodom's sin. God's destruction of Sodom and Gomorrah served as a warning that society holds a sacred responsibility in rooting out this sin, seeking always to abolish this act from within their midst.

Because of the deadly consequences caused by tolerance toward Sodom's sin, it is important to correctly define what the sin of Sodom actually is.

Genesis 19 opens with the two angels, sent to Sodom to bring about its destruction, finding lodging at Lot's house. But a frightening and terrifying scene unfolds before Lot's guests settle down for the evening. The young and old men of the town surround the house, and banging on the door, they demand that the strangers be handed over to them so that they can know them ("to know" being a euphemism for having a sexual relationship).

Women are absent as men demand that the foreigners be turned over to them. The demand from Sodom's men to rape the two strangers has led many interpreters of this text, over the centuries, to associate homosexuality with Sodom's sin. So ingrained is this interpretation that we have come to accept it as true. Yet to claim that homosexuality is the sin of Sodom is problematic. Linking this biblical passage to homosexuality is complicated if we recognize that no specific equivalent exists in the Hebrew (or Greek) text for the word *homosexual*. No biblical word exists whose meaning remotely defines the essence of how the contemporary word *homosexuality* is used. The Hebrew text, as well as the Greek, uses idioms making any interpretation of the passage difficult. The term *homosexual* did not even come into existence among English speakers until the nineteenth century. The word *sodomy*, derived from the town's name and associated with its supposed sin, did not enter the English language until the thirteenth century, and even then the word was not always connected with intercourse between men, as it is today. In different historical periods, *sodomy* has meant everything from anal copulation among men, to acts of heterosexual oral sex, to bestiality. Hence, a danger exists in juxtaposing ancient biblical prohibitions with contemporary sexual milieus without considering the historical and cultural social location from which these prohibitions arose.

Relying on the biblical text to determine what Sodom's sin was makes homosexuality an even more unlikely candidate. While it is true that in several places throughout the Scriptures Sodom has come to signify evil and rebellion, nowhere does the Bible refer to or link homosexuality to Sodom. What, then, is the sin of Sodom that societies must protect themselves against, lest the wrath of God be unleashed? Commenting on Sodom's sin, the prophet Ezekiel wrote that Sodom's iniquity was the city residents' unwillingness, due to their pride and haughtiness, to share their abundance with those who were poor and marginalized.[1] It is this haughtiness that becomes the root cause of the abomination they participated in before the eyes of God. Amos prophesied the destruction of Israel for following Sodom's example of oppressing the needy and crushing the poor.[2] For the prophet Isaiah, Israel is referred to as Sodom and Gomorrah because it was committing the same acts that led to the destruction of those cities. The prophet states, "Hear the word of the LORD, you rulers of Sodom! Listen to the teaching of our God, you people of Gomorrah! . . . Your hands are full of blood. Wash yourselves; make yourselves clean; remove the evil of your doings from before my eyes; cease to do evil, learn to do good; seek justice, rescue the oppressed, defend the orphan, plead for the widow" (Isa 1:10, 15–17). Israel's sin, like that of Sodom and Gomorrah, is a lack of justice done in the name of the orphans and widows. Within patriarchal societies, the most vulnerable members are those who are not under the care of a man, specifically the orphan who has lost her or his father and the widow who has lost her husband. Deprived of a male protector, they cease to hold any standing in a male-centered society. For this reason the Bible makes their care the responsibility of all.

Early rabbinical writings attested that throughout early Judaism, a link did not exist between Sodom's sin and homosexuality. According to the Babylonian Talmud, "Our Rabbis taught: The men of Sodom waxed haughty only on account of the good which the Holy One, blessed be He, had lavished upon them . . . They said: Since there cometh forth bread out of [our] earth, and it hath the dust of gold, why should we suffer wayfarers, who come to us only to deplete our wealth. Come, let us abolish the practice of traveling in our land."[3]

The first instance of defining Sodom's sin as a homosexual act occurred centuries later. The Jewish philosopher Philo of Alexandria (c. 25 BCE to 50 CE) wrote, "But God, having taken pity on mankind, as being a Savior and

---

1. See Ezek 16:49.
2. Amos 4:1, 11.
3. *Sanhedrin* 109a.

full of love for mankind, increased, as far as possible, the natural desire of men and women for a connection together, for the sake of producing children, and detesting the unnatural and unlawful commerce of the people of Sodom, he extinguished it, and destroyed those who were inclined to these things."[4] Likewise, Josephus (c. 37–100 CE), who was commissioned by Roman authorities to write the history of the Jews, wrote, "Now when the Sodomites saw the young men to be of beautiful countenances, and this to an extraordinary degree . . . they resolved themselves to enjoy these beautiful boys by force and violence."[5]

The sin of Sodom, as defined by the biblical text and the early rabbinical writings, does not refer to a loving relationship between two individuals of the same sex. What, then, is the sin of Sodom and Gomorrah? What is the sin in which many political and religious leaders today participate? Throughout the biblical text, in every passage in which Sodom's wickedness is mentioned, homosexuality is never given as the cause for God's wrath. Such an interpretation came centuries later. The sin of Sodom and Gomorrah, according to the Bible, was a lack of justice done in the name of the dispossessed. God's anger consumes Sodom and Gomorrah because of the dominant culture's refusal to show hospitality to those residing on the margins.

In the biblical world, hospitality meant more than simply being neighborly; it was a carefully orchestrated social practice to receive strangers and make them guests. Strangers, lacking legal standing, were at the mercy of established community leaders who were willing to serve as their host. Their very survival would depend on falling under the protection of a member of the town. Throughout the Bible, prophets remind God's people of these ancient traditions, warning them that hospitality was to be extended to the marginalized. Dishonoring the orphan, the widow, the alien—in short, those who were disenfranchised—signified a godless nation liable to God's wrath. This is why Jesus, as he gave instructions to his disciples preparing to embark on a missionary journey, stated that those cities that refused them hospitality would suffer a fate worse than Sodom.[6]

Rather than using this passage to condemn homosexuality, it would be more biblically sound to refer to this story in condemning how First World nations economically treat the peoples of Third World nations,

---

4. Philo of Alexandria, *On Abraham*, 27.137.
5. Josephus, *Antiquities of the Jews*, 1.11.3.
6. See Luke 10:1–12.

which is not so different from what the Sodomites hoped to do to the aliens in their own midst. Today, inhabitants of First World nations exhibit the same xenophobia demonstrated by the Sodomites. Like the residents of Sodom, who sought to physically rape the foreigners in their midst, we today economically rape the poor and the undocumented alien. In ancient Sodom, those in power desired to subordinate the stranger; in the United States today, some desire to do the same to the undocumented and the alien in our midst. To cite a recent example, Arizona Senate Bill 1070 has more to do with the sin of Sodom than does a same-gender loving relationship.

If readers today insist on associating Sodom's sin with a sexual act, then the only argument that could feasibly be made is that same-gender gang rape perpetrated by heterosexual men is wrong. Even then, rape is not a sexual act, even though it is a violence involving sexual organs. Rape is foremost an act of domination in which pleasure is achieved through the humiliation and subjugation of the victim. Lot's daughters became unsatisfactory substitutes for the purpose of sexual abuse because the goal of Sodom's men was not to quench sexual appetites but to dominate and domesticate the strangers within their midst. The desire of mortal men to rape "heavenly messengers" was the desire to subjugate the things of heaven to the will of humans. It was an assault on God's authority! The sin of Sodom is not homosexuality but unchecked heterosexuality, that is, the attempt to dominate everything, to subject everything, even the things of God, to the male penis. Let us remember that the two strangers were not humans but angels; sexual intercourse with heavenly beings by humans would be a transgression of the natural order. Passages in the New Testament that refer to Sodom's sin and God's punishment for their "shameless ways" and "unnatural fornication" (i.e., 2 Pet 2:4–8 and Jude 7) begin to make sense. Obviously, the authors of these New Testament books were not referring to our modern understanding of homosexual orientation.

Many years have passed since Tommy and I were buddies. I married and moved away from Miami. Hurricane Andrew hit and I lost touch with almost all of my church friends. Still, I often think of Tommy. I sincerely regret the additional spiritual burdens that I placed upon him due to my biblical ignorance and naiveté. Rather than sharing the good news that God loves him just as God created him, I added to his sense of self-loathing. How I wish I would have shared that because all that God creates is good, he should never settle for being "tolerated." Like all humans, he should be woven into the tapestry of society. It is one thing for some heterosexuals to disagree with homosexuals or question their orientation; it is another for those heterosexuals to use their power within society, which is derived from their heterosexual privilege, to impose their views and, in doing so, deny the humanness of others, including Tommy. And we who are heterosexual should learn that our orientation, like that of homosexuals, is but a part of who we are, not the totality of our identity. Those who are homosexual are more than gay; they are parents, siblings, children, teachers, scientists, ministers, politicians, military personnel, and world leaders. For not sharing this good news I will remain eternally sorry. I will always be grateful for the role Tommy unwittingly played in my own conversion, my becoming a person who is now committed to issues of justice for all who are disenfranchised.

# 21

# The Bible Says It . . . I Believe It . . . That Settles It?

## Glen Miles

The Reverend Dr. Glen Miles is the senior minister of Country Club Christian Church (Disciples of Christ) in Kansas City, Missouri, where he preached the following sermon on August 5, 2012. An ordained minister in the Christian Church (Disciples of Christ), Dr. Miles has served as a community organizer and denominational leader in a variety of capacities and was recently elected as the moderator for the Disciples of Christ. He also has written a book for preachers, titled *Between Gloom and Glory*.

---

*Ephesians 4:1–16*

In 1969 there was a huge controversy in the church I attended with my family.

The Vietnam War was raging, but that wasn't the issue.

There was a movement called free love, but that wasn't it either.

Our country was faced with all sorts of concerns, but the one I remember, the one that caused a huge argument in that congregation, was whether or not a woman could wear pants to church.

"Women wearing pants is a sign of disrespect to God," someone said.

## Part Four: Calling for Transformation

The controversy raged for a while until the preacher's wife, who also happened to be my mom, showed up in pants. People talked. Some wondered out loud what was happening to our church. But the next Sunday half the women showed up wearing pants and suddenly the issue died away.

Fifteen years later, in 1984, I applied for a part-time job at a church in California where I hoped to work while I was in seminary. During the interview, they asked my opinion on women in ministry. I was honest in my reply. I said, "I believe women can serve as deacons, elders and pastors. There are no barriers." A woman on the search committee, the wife of the senior minister, said, "Women serving communion would be too distracting. I'd be looking at their outfits and not thinking about our Lord." I replied, flippantly, "Well, I've been distracted by some really ugly ties worn by male elders." At that moment, I noticed one of the men on the committee was wearing the ugliest orange and black tie I have ever seen. I didn't get the job.

These stories are rather quaint and silly in hindsight but I can assure you, the issue of women in ministry was a huge controversy at the time for the church. Sadly, it is still a concern for some congregations and individual Christians.

Here in Kansas City, Country Club Christian Church was considered a trailblazer in the 1930s when women were allowed to share in Sunday school class leadership. Back in the 1980s, this church elected its first woman to chair the congregational board. This congregation has hired several ordained women to serve as ministers. That women in church leadership positions was a huge concern in the our recent past is almost hard to believe today. We've been very clear about the full inclusion of women in ministry but we still encounter some who oppose that idea.

There have been a few occasions here when a couple getting married in our sanctuary has come to me to request a male minister. These folks are not members of our church. They usually begin by saying something like, "We like this church because you welcome everyone. You must surely understand that in our background we have male ministers only, and we'd like to request one of the male ministers here to help with the wedding." I make it clear that we make assignments based on our schedules and that we don't change our plan simply because the couple prefers male over female for their minister. I also make it clear that we do not change this policy because to do so would imply that we no longer support women in ministry.

These haven't always been pleasant conversations, but we remain steadfast in our understanding that God calls both women and men into ministry.

Throughout the history of the church, local congregations have had to wrestle with potentially divisive issues. When Paul wrote his letter to Ephesus, there was a controversy facing the church, one that almost split it from the beginning. The concern was circumcision. The church was expanding into Gentile communities, and there were some who were certain that the church must retain the practice of circumcision. Like the stories about women in ministry, this problem seems silly now. But at the time it was very serious.

There were those who interpreted the issue of circumcision in a traditional way. The practice was a longstanding part of their faith community. Their fathers, grandfathers, and great-grandfathers had all participated in this ritual. Heck, they could even trace it all the way back to Moses! Talk about an enduring tradition.

Paul, however, saw the tradition as a barrier, a wall, and a separation. He recognized that it had become not a theological issue but a cultural one, and he knew that in order for the church to move forward, they had to learn how to reinterpret the Bible and what it said about circumcision. They had to reinterpret it in order to keep from splitting.

As The Message rendering of this passage describes, the author of this letter encourages them to "travel on the same road and in the same direction . . . both outwardly and inwardly. You have one master, one faith, one baptism, one God . . . Everything you are is permeated with oneness."

Paul is preaching unity and oneness. This unity was a big deal. That the Ephesian church was thriving was due to its ability to understand the old story in the new light of Christ. Their oneness didn't mean that they all looked and spoke and acted the same. It meant that they saw that they were united under the grace and love of God. That grace, that love, defined who they were, and nothing else.

In today's church, especially the church in the U.S., we could use a good dose of this gracious unity. We could use a good reminder of Jesus' teaching that all of the laws—including Leviticus and Deuteronomy, ancient books that still are quoted today—are encompassed by the law of love for God and for neighbor. We could take a lesson from this story because today there are loud voices in our culture calling for us to return to the traditional, biblical view of marriage. It is time for us to reinterpret some of the old traditional views on marriage.

## Part Four: Calling for Transformation

You may be surprised to learn this but the best place to go to discover how to do this is the Bible itself. Since we are followers of Jesus, let's start with a story from his life. In the Gospel of John we learn about a woman who was caught in adultery. She was brought before Jesus by a group of religious scholars and leaders. They said to him, "Teacher, this woman was caught in the very act of committing adultery. Now [the Bible] commanded us to stone such women. Now what do you say?" (John 8:4–5).

They know that if he says, "The Bible says it, I believe it, that settles it—go ahead and stone her," then they will put her to death, and he won't be very popular among his followers. They also know that if he ignores the Bible, at least the way they are interpreting it, he will get into serious trouble with the religious leaders and lawyers, who will have grounds to accuse him of blasphemy and much worse.

It's a sneak attack. They don't care about the woman. They don't care about the law. They're just trying to trap Jesus.

Jesus responds by refusing to allow narrow-minded legalism and biblical literalism to determine his answer. He sees what is happening. These are angry men. They have rocks in their hands and they're ready to let 'em fly in order to make their point. But Jesus instead reinterprets the moment through grace, forgiveness, and love. He looks to the crowd and says, "If there is one of you without sin, well then, go ahead, throw your stone."

That answer didn't come from Leviticus. It wasn't part of the traditional understanding. It wasn't in their Bibles. Jesus, in that moment, reinterpreted that old law.

That is what grace is about. It is not about being lenient. It is not about ignoring foolish behaviors and immoral acts. It is about naming the issue so we can face it and learn to grow up. The last paragraph of our reading today basically says that "God wants us to grow up"! Grace requires us to bring a grown-up mentality to the traditions and teachings that have been part of our church for thousands of years. In the story of the woman caught in adultery, Jesus refuses to be lead into the trap of simplistic thinking. He knows the Bible as well as the ones standing before him, but instead of falling back on the old "the Bible says it, I believe it, that settles it" routine that so many, even today, seem to think is the right way or most convenient way to interpret it, he puts them into the middle of the interpretive action. He does not interpret it traditionally. He reinterprets it in the light of love.

"Whoever is without sin . . . go ahead and throw the first stone."

The story says that the angry mob, beginning with the oldest men first, put down their stones and walked away.

Have you ever held a rock in your hand? Have you ever come to church ready to judge, ready to condemn, while avoiding your own issues, your own concerns and weaknesses? The church finds it easy to attack the sins of the flesh, but what about the sins of the spirit?

Jesus' audience on that day would have seen the angry men as righteous and the woman as a sinner. Jesus makes it clear that they are one in their failings.

The story is one of redemption. The woman is certainly redeemed. She has made a mistake or, more likely, she has been forced into a sinful act against her will. First-century Palestine was a patriarchal society. Women were treated like property. Women were often used by men, then thrown aside. But Jesus treats her not like property or an object; rather, he treats her as a human being made in the image of God.

The real redemption is taking place among the men. Their recognition of their own failings and their need for grace as much as the woman—maybe even more than her—is their first step toward a redeemed life, a new life, a change in behavior in the here and now. Salvation in its purest and most realistic form.

Buzz Thomas, a Baptist preacher, once said that "life, properly told, is a redemption story." I once heard him preach a sermon in which he told a story about former U.S. president Bill Clinton. Clinton had delivered a speech to the Texas state legislature. After the speech there was a question-and-answer session. One legislator asked the former president about placing the Ten Commandments in the public square. Clinton began by saying, "Well, as the world's most famous sinner, let me say this . . ."

That is a step toward redemption. That is a step toward living under grace.

The recognition of the need for grace is the single most powerful principle in the church. No one—not your pastor, not the chair of the elders, not the chair of our board, not the most respected member of our faith community—no one can stand at the Lord's table without the gracious invitation of God.

In fact, I think this story was included in the New Testament as a warning and a reminder to the early church and to every church, to every person since then, to put down our rocks, to leave our condemnations aside

PART FOUR: CALLING FOR TRANSFORMATION

and see every person as a child in need of the love of God. This recognition leads to unity.

I've told you this story to make two points: one, Jesus modeled the way we are to interpret the Bible. As followers of Christ, as ones who take the name Christian, we are instructed by his life—the way he lived and the way he taught—how to understand the Bible.

He taught that all of the commandments are understood and interpreted through the single commandment of loving God and loving neighbor, which is also the commandment at the heart of the Torah. He refuses to allow the traditional view to dominate his thinking. Instead, he almost uses that law of love of God and love of neighbor like a colander, one that allows you to rinse away all of the things that don't matter while you keep the important stuff. It's almost as if that's what Jesus does with this law. The law of love is a colander that allows us to see things more clearly, to keep what really matters most. We can learn a lot from his approach.

So what about all of this talk in the news recently about a traditional understanding of marriage and what the Bible teaches about this? If we are going to be honest in this conversation, then we need to note that there is no singular teaching in the Bible about marriage. In fact, I could easily use the Bible, in a very traditional style, to prove that polygamy and the keeping of concubines is an acceptable practice. I could argue for forcing a widow to marry her husband's brother, especially if she and her husband did not yet have children.

We could make a case for all kinds of things that would get us in trouble if we approached the Bible in a traditional style. I could use the Bible, including the New Testament, to argue in favor of slavery. A traditional reading could easily conclude that keeping slaves is acceptable. Paul wrote, "Slaves, obey your masters" (Col 3:22). But as a nation we figured out 150 years ago that a traditional understanding of the Bible was allowing a horrific practice to take place.

We were able to see that we're invited to read the entire Bible through the lens, through the colander, of love, so that the things that matter least can be washed away, and with the eyes of love, we can see what matters the most.

The second reason I am telling you this is connected to today's reading from Ephesians. As I noted, the church in Ephesus, many years before this letter was written, was almost torn apart by the issue of circumcision. There were some who clung to the traditional biblical view of the idea of circumcision. Looking back two thousand years later, it seems kind of silly. Really, the church almost split over this cultural thing? Yes, they almost did. That's why today's reading makes it clear that we're called to work together toward unity. Toward walking on the same road together, to being mature in the way we handle these conversations.

Here's the thing. The church will constantly be challenged by cultural changes. Two hundred years ago no one would have dreamed of walking into a church and seeing a woman in the pulpit. The conversations in our world, especially in our country and in our churches, about the traditional understanding of marriage are heated, they're strong, and they're angry. But when we look at controversial issues as a unified body of Christ, through the lens of grace, through the colander of love . . . Can we see that whatever the issue before us, we are called to be united in our desire to love God, to love neighbor? That is the only rule we need.

# 22

# The Coherent and the Contingent

## Eric Elnes

The Reverend Dr. Eric Elnes is an author, biblical scholar, and ordained minister in the United Church of Christ who hosts the popular Internet show *Darkwood Brew*. He is the author of several books, most notably *Asphalt Jesus* and *The Phoenix Affirmations*. He holds a PhD in biblical studies from Princeton Theological Seminary. This is the second in a series of sermons related to faith and homosexuality that he preached at Countryside Community Church in Omaha, Nebraska, where he serves as senior minister. The first explored the story of Peter and Cornelius as reflected in Acts 10–11.

---

*Leviticus 18:22; 20:8–18* · *1 Corinthians 7:10–15*

## I. A "Biblical" Faith

Last week we asked the question, "What does a 'biblical' faith look like?" Does having a "biblical" faith mean that you read the Bible as God's literal, inerrant Word? What we found is that, by this definition, the Apostle Peter would not even come close to having a "biblical" faith. When we stop trying to define what "biblical" would be on our own and turn to the Bible itself for guidance, we find that the faith actually in the Bible looks quite different than that proposed by fundamentalist Christianity. It also looks quite different from liberal Christianity, by the way, which essentially proposes that we write off the Bible as little more than primitive superstition.

Peter was a serious student of the Scriptures. It is quite evident that Peter's whole world was infused with, and informed by, Scripture. Yet drawing from Peter as an example of what it means to have a "biblical" faith, we must conclude that the Holy Spirit trumps Scripture. If the Holy Spirit directs you to eat foods that are clearly prohibited in Scripture, for instance, Peter would advise you to fire up the barbecue. If the Holy Spirit directs you to associate yourself with people whom Scripture clearly forbids you to associate with, or the Spirit instructs you to allow these same people into full fellowship within your faith community, Peter would advise that you open the door wide and embrace them no matter what Scripture says.

Now, some of you are probably cheering right about now about the Holy Spirit trumping Scripture, and some of you are worrying. To those of you who are cheering, I suggest that you've got something to worry about. And to those of you who are worrying, you have more reason for comfort than you may think.

If you're cheering, bear in mind that it's no easy task to determine what the Holy Spirit is saying. Last fall we spent six weeks asking how we know if it's the Holy Spirit talking and not the pizza we just ate. We could have spent six months, even six years, refining that topic. It takes a lot of work to discern whether something's coming from the Spirit or another source. In our fast food culture, we generally resist putting in the time it takes to develop an affinity for discernment. We seek quick-fix solutions—like pulling a line from Scripture out of context and applying it to any given situation.

## II. Picking and Choosing

Let's consider a quick-fix approach for a moment, shall we? Let's read some Scripture and see how it may speak to our lives today. Consider our passage from Lev 20:8–18. I've been preaching and teaching about faith and homosexuality for more than fifteen years, and I must confess to being awfully tired of having to defend LGBTQ people against the claims made in Leviticus 18. I say this as a straight person. If you're straight, too, imagine how a gay person feels, especially to hear the call for the death penalty.

So I'd like to put others on the hot seat for a change. The passage above deals with more than just "men who lay with men." Let's focus instead on

PART FOUR: CALLING FOR TRANSFORMATION

the children, particularly the children who disrespect us parents. (Now here's a passage we can apply directly from "God's Word" in Scripture!) Why shouldn't we pay more attention to the need to stone our disrespectful children to death than to the gays? After all, there are all kinds of gay people who are the nicest, most respectful, just, and upright people you'll ever meet. Why would we want to stone these folks? What have they ever done to us? But in the case of disrespectful children, each and every one of them is being punished for a sin they've actually committed against us. Deuteronomy 21 gives us permission to stone them not just for cursing, but for showing any sign of rebellion or refusing to obey their parents. While we're on the subject of rebellious children, we might as well add that the next chapter in Deuteronomy also gives us permission to stone teenage girls who have sex before marriage.

Now, let me add that the Bible does allow for a way to have sex before marriage and live to tell about it. If you are unmarried and are raped, you won't get stoned. And the Bible commands your rapist to marry you and never get divorced. And fathers, bear in mind that the rapist must pay you fifty shekels of silver for dishonoring your name.

What?! You have a problem with God's Word? But this is God's Word every bit as much as the Leviticus saying about "men lying with men" is God's Word. Don't tell me you're picking and choosing Scripture to suit your interests...

The fact of the matter is that the Bible clearly forbids that which even the most conservative, Bible-believing Christian would permit. In fact, in light of what the Bible says, the most conservative among us would seem like wild-eyed hedonist libertines. For instance, the Bible prohibits the following:

- weaving two kinds of cloth together (Lev 19:19);
- mixing two kinds of grain together (Lev 19:19);
- crossbreeding animals (Lev 19:19);
- marrying outside the faith (Deut 7:1–4; Ezra 10:2–3; 1 Cor 7:39);
- remarrying after a divorce (Mark 10:10–12);
- having sex at "that time of month"; the couple is to be cut off forever from their community (Lev 20:18);
- eating pork (Lev 11:7) or shellfish (Lev 11:10);

- and, most disconcerting for us Nebraska Huskers football fans, touching the skin of a pig (Lev 11:8).

Lest you think I'm being all sanctimonious, consider me as a clergyperson. The Bible clearly states you may not become clergy if you

- trim your beard or sideburns;
- marry a nonvirgin, widow, or divorcee;
- have a limb that's too long or short;
- happen to be too thin or too small (I like those two!);
- have defective eyesight;
- happen to be hunchbacked;
- have skin disease;
- have damaged testicles.[1]

I was never asked about any of these things on my ordination exams. Even more surprising, I was never even asked if I had been a banker or had money in an interest-bearing savings account! What? You're not familiar with what the Bible says about that? There are so many injunctions in the Bible against charging interest that it's laughable that the banks aren't being picketed by Christians every week carrying signs that say, "God hates loan officers!"

In the book of Ezekiel, as one of many "for instances," those who charge interest on loans are lumped in with murderers, robbers, adulterers, and idolaters, and are said to be worthy of death.[2] Shouldn't we at least be proposing that bankers go to jail, and to make interest-bearing accounts illegal? Or are you going to be all liberal-y now that it affects you?

Then again, maybe the Bible itself could stand to be stricter. After all, it not only prohibits things that even the most conservative among us would permit, but it permits things that even the most conservative among us would prohibit. Like polygamy. And slavery. And treating women like property.

---

1. See Lev 21 for rules concerning the holiness of priests.
2. See Ezek 18:10–13.

Part Four: Calling for Transformation

## III. The Coherent and the Contingent

What are we to do with all of this if we are to have a "biblical" faith? The fact of the matter is that everyone who takes the Bible seriously, no matter how conservative or liberal, has a "canon within a canon." Certain parts of Scripture speak with more authority than other parts. So, for instance, when Peter claimed to have a vision from the Holy Spirit that revealed that it was okay to eat non-kosher foods and to baptize Gentiles into the faith, that revelation formed part of Peter's own canon within a canon. Certain Scriptures no longer spoke with the authority they once had. And certain other Scriptures spoke with more authority. The fact that Peter's conclusions started resonating with more and more people in the Christian community lent further credence to his vision, to the point where it became the "orthodox" position.

Biblical scholars sometimes speak about separating the coherent from the contingent when it comes to privileging certain Scriptures over others. The Bible contains writings that span more than one thousand years. Certain themes within Scripture seem to appear and reappear over and over regardless of time period or cultural context. These themes give the Bible a coherent voice. On the other hand, other themes seem to appear far less often, being more contingent upon a particular time period and cultural setting. One generation says something that is not echoed by the next generation.

To give a concrete example: there are three great law codes in the Hebrew Bible—the Holiness Code (Lev 17–26), the Covenant Code (Exod 20–23), and the Deuteronomic Code (Deut 12–26). Each of these law codes was written during a different time period, and each seems to be an attempt by a distinct generation of Israelites to interpret in their day how to live by the Ten Commandments. Some of the laws contradict each other; many of them reflect vastly different ideas of what is important.

Isn't it interesting that at one point in Israel's history, people came to the conclusion that an earlier law code wasn't working for them and so wrote a new one? Later, others looked back and concluded that neither of the two law codes was working for them and wrote a third. In terms of coherence and contingence, one can see that the coherence behind the law codes is the Ten Commandments. The contingencies are the precise laws themselves, which change according to the present understanding of the people.

## IV. Paul's "Biblical" Faith

The Apostle Paul models what it is like to have a "biblical" faith that is able to separate the coherence from the contingencies of Scripture. One particularly telling place he models this sensitivity is in his advice about divorce. (Sorry to put the divorcees on the hot seat again, but perhaps you now know a little of what it's like to be gay . . .) In 1 Cor 7:10–15, Paul answers a question about divorce this way:

> To the married I give this command—not I but the Lord—that the wife should not separate from her husband (but if she does separate, let her remain unmarried or else be reconciled to her husband), and that the husband should not divorce his wife. To the rest I say—I and not the Lord—that if any believer has a wife who is an unbeliever, and she consents to live with him, he should not divorce her. And if any woman has a husband who is an unbeliever, and he consents to live with her, she should not divorce him. For the unbelieving husband is made holy through his wife, and the unbelieving wife is made holy through her husband. Otherwise, your children would be unclean, but as it is, they are holy. But if the unbelieving partner separates, let it be so; in such a case the brother or sister is not bound. It is to peace that God has called you.

Do you find it curious that Paul directly contradicts Jesus' own teaching on divorce? It's obvious that Paul knows what Jesus says (he cites Jesus), then he makes it clear that he is going to give different advice ("I and not the Lord"). How can you directly contradict Jesus, allowing for divorce in circumstances for which Jesus has clearly made no such exception?[3]

Paul tells us how. He appeals to the fact that God has called us to "peace," or what in Hebrew would have been called Shalom. Shalom doesn't just mean "peace" as in absence of fighting. Shalom means peace as a form of wholeness, health, and flourishing.

You see, while Scripture holds marriage in high esteem, and has something negative to say about divorce, it holds Shalom in far higher esteem than marriage. If you look at the whole thrust of Scripture, Shalom is one of the highest values you can find there. Peace, health, wholeness, and prospering are what allow a person not merely to survive but to thrive. So if you are in a marriage but do not have Shalom, you are not

---

3. For Jesus' comments on divorce, see especially Matt 5:31–32; 19:1–12; Mark 10:2–12; Luke 16:18.

in a "biblical" marriage. Breaking up a marriage doesn't necessarily lead to "peace, health, wholeness, and prospering" either. But Paul recognized that in certain circumstances the chances are higher that one will achieve Shalom and will thrive by breaking marriage bonds than by maintaining a bad marriage just for the sake of staying married.

In Scripture, Shalom is the deep, coherent ripple effect that spreads ever outward. It comes from God's desire that each of us should not just survive this earthly life but should thrive here. Every generation from the biblical era to this day has encountered this ripple effect that enables a wider and wider circle of people to find Shalom and to thrive. The ripple has sometimes "made waves," causing entire communities to reevaluate their life together and the basic rules by which they govern themselves. In the Hebrew Bible alone we know there were at least three such periods. Could we be in another such period now? Could it be that part of what is causing chaos and infighting, in the Christian community and beyond, over a number of faith issues is that we are responding to another of God's ripples that is producing waves, moving us to widen our circle of welcome and compassion?

Only time will tell. But whether we are responding to God's ripple or simply taking the next small step together on the journey of faith, we may at least acknowledge that we are more entangled with one another than we often suspect. The fate of the rebellious teen is tied to that of the divorcee; the fate of the banker is tied to that of the clergyperson who doesn't fit the Levitical mold, as well as that of the homosexual couple—all are bound together. The ability of each group to thrive in this world depends, in part, on the faith community exercising a truly "biblical" faith instead of a "biblical" faith in appearance only. Our responsibility—and joy—as Christians is to sort out the coherent from the contingent in Scripture with the Holy Spirit's guidance. Based on what we find there, we are to embody the ethics of Shalom, that the ripples of God's love and grace may continue to extend further and further into a world that yearns to hear—and experience—the good news.

# 23

# Text and Taboo

## Tad DeLay

Tad DeLay is a PhD student studying philosophy of religion at Claremont School of Theology and is the author of *God Is Unconscious: Psychoanalysis and Theology*. He also holds an MA in theology and biblical studies from Fuller Theological Seminary. This sermon was originally preached at Fuller Theological Seminary on May 21, 2012, and was adapted for publication. Before beginning seminary, Tad lost his job as a pastor in Arkansas when his views began to shift toward full inclusion and equality of LGBTQ people in the church.

---

*Acts 10:1–33*

Let me begin with a word about ideologies, paradigms, and communal beliefs. These are terms I'm using for whatever authorizes views and behaviors that keep us from seeing ourselves through the eyes of the other, that legitimate our prejudices as being okay even when they're unhelpful and unhealthy for everybody involved. Ideology is the basic posture remaining in power even without the supports of our arguments. Regardless of our best intentions, communal beliefs reinforce the other's status as *taboo*.

The story of Peter and Cornelius is a way to talk about unconscious biases—ideologies, paradigms, communal beliefs—that believe for us, on our behalf, without our realizing it. It is the sentiment that says, "I personally don't judge [x], but nevertheless Scripture says . . ." For example, "I personally don't judge gays and lesbians, but nevertheless Scripture says it's wrong, so I'm against it." In other words, "I don't believe personally, but my [religion, sacred book, pastor, church, etc.] believes for me." All of which gets a person off the hook.

In Acts 10, Peter initially justifies his lack of interaction with the Gentiles (those outside of his community) not by his personal opinion but by the Torah itself. ("I have never eaten anything that is profane or unclean!") And it took a vision from God, experienced three times, to change his mind about the Gentiles. But just a few chapters later, when he reneges on his commitment to the Gentiles at the behest of his more conservative cohort in Jerusalem (see Acts 15 as read through the eyes of Paul in Galatians 2—more about this later), it took a human act to convince him that the way he continued his practice of excluding Gentiles could not be justified.

Now, let's pay attention to a few subtleties in this text. When called by Cornelius, a Roman centurion and Gentile, Peter was staying at the house of a tanner. We cannot infer much, but why is this mentioned? By trade, a tanner works with dead animal skins. If this tanner goes to synagogue or participates at all in the temple rituals, he likely has to keep a very rigid schedule to make sure he is ritually clean. By contrast, of course, Peter is clean—he makes that abundantly clear ("I have never eaten anything that is profane or unclean!")—but he is staying with someone who is perpetually in a state of uncleanliness.

Why would Peter do this? I wonder if he, like so many contemporary Christians, sees himself as being edgy. "I am clean, but I have a friend who is a tanner." How does Peter see himself in relation to the people he's going to interact with? Does he flirt with the line while maintaining the taboo? Kind of like those who are quick to say they have lots of close friends who are gay, but their religion doesn't allow them to condone such a "lifestyle"? Peter does not need a well-developed argument for why he does not interact with the Gentiles. His belief believes for him. His community believes for him. His Scripture believes for him. His paradigm can account for anything (fragile though it may be).

The story concludes with Peter effectively saying to Cornelius and his household, "You understand, right? It is against our Scriptures for me to visit you." Entering the house of the Gentile transgressed his moral norms not simply in Peter's opinion but according to the very plain text itself. The vision he experienced three times told him to do the opposite of the text, and Peter eventually makes an exception in the direction of progress. But as Paul in his letter to the Galatians makes clear, Peter's progress is short-lived.

I grew up in Little Rock, Arkansas. We still talk about the Little Rock Nine and the integration of Central High School in 1957. The Supreme Court had struck down "separate but equal" in the 1954 case *Brown v. Board of Education*. By the time the city submitted a plan to integrate, segregationists stood ready to protest. On the first day of the school year in September 1957, nine African American students approached the school to learn Governor Orval Faubus had mobilized the National Guard—men with assault weapons—to block the entrance to the school. The mayor petitioned the White House to intervene, and President Eisenhower commandeered the troops, ordering them to stay at the school to ensure the African American students could enter the school safely.

The problem only escalated. There are unbelievably vicious pictures and horrific stories from those days, pure hatred doubtlessly disguised in the esoteric language of religious people angry at a government contravening God's moral order of segregation. One African American girl was locked in a restroom stall while her white classmates set the stall on fire. Acid was thrown in another student's eyes. And instead of continuing with the integration, the governor shut down the entire Little Rock school district for the 1958 year.

Listen: do you think anybody experiences himself as racist?

In Acts 10, does Peter think of himself as a bigot? Bigotry is not typically something we consciously experience in ourselves. Our ideologies, paradigms, and communal beliefs justify it for us. We see bigotry in others, in actions, and in the systemic operations of society. But nobody thinks of herself as a horrible person with an irrational hatred of others.

It's not that Peter is a villain. It's not that he has a well-crafted argument that ends up being indefensible. Peter simply has Torah, a community, and a paradigm that he has always operated out of without having to experience the antagonism of shifting his belief about the Other—about someone he has been taught is taboo. His rules have allowed him to operate unconsciously, on autopilot.

A few chapters later we find Peter at the Jerusalem council giving account for his actions with the Gentiles. Paul pulls back the veil to tell us what happened at that council. Peter and Paul had a confrontation. Paul came to Peter and said something to the effect of, "You were known as the leader who would actually eat with Gentiles, and that was a big deal! But to please James and his conservative crowd, you gave up. You didn't object to God in the first place, but in the end you did."

It was the text, the ego, and the community. How does perception block us from seeing things right in front of us? I once could see, but now I'm blind.

Why did Peter revert to his previous practices?

Was it those same biases that he grew up with that derailed his progress? "Those people," and so on . . .

Was it his desire to be a responsible pastor sensitive to his congregation? "I have to think of the more conservative members on my board . . ."

We do not ultimately know whether Peter took Paul's advice. Where did it go from there? And if Peter did change (again), why did it take an act of man beyond the divine revelation to move him beyond his prejudices?

If the heavens were to open three times and reveal all truth to me, would that not be enough for me to change? Or is this what happens when I am convinced the gods already agree with me, because I can surely prove it with an unquestionable text?

Are the false gods of our ideologies really that strong? What causes us to object even when we secretly know how stories of prejudice end? What monster have we fed that can overrule everything else around us?

# 24

# Rolling Back the Stone

## Holly E. Hearon

The Reverend Dr. Holly E. Hearon is a minister of word and sacrament in the Presbyterian Church (USA) who is T. J. and Virginia Liggett Professor of Christian Traditions and Professor of New Testament Emerita at Christian Theological Seminary in Indianapolis, Indiana, where a version of this sermon was preached on April 3, 2013. An award-winning author, her publications include *The Mary Magdalene Tradition: Witness and Counter-Witness in Early Christian Communities*.

---

### John 20:19–23

"When it was evening on that day, the first day of the week"—the same day that Mary Magdalene had gone to the tomb alone and seen the risen Jesus with her own eyes and heard his voice—"the doors of the house where the disciples had met were locked for fear of the Jews" (John 20:19).

This is not an auspicious beginning for the post-resurrection community. How is it that the disciples have moved from the tomb, where the stone has been rolled away—a tomb not unlike that from which Jesus called Lazarus forth from death to life—to a room where the doors are locked shut? Threatened with resurrection, it is as if they have chosen to reenter the tomb and roll the stone back over the door.

John says it was because of fear. Fear is a powerful emotion. It is also an important emotion: it can alert us to when danger is present—when something or *someone* threatens our well-being and brings us to the edge of the cliff that separates life from death. Sometimes it is a literal death, when we are faced with violence or disease; sometimes an emotional death, when, for example, we lose a job, or a relationship falls apart, or we are forced to make a change not of our own choosing.

But fear is a complex emotion. By creating an atmosphere of fear, people can use fear to control us, so that we are afraid to speak or act in any way that might inch us closer to the edge of that cliff. And when we are trapped in a state of fear, specters can arise before our eyes, so that we begin to see threats where none exist.

In the case of the disciples, John says that they are in hiding because of fear of the Jews. A better translation might be "Judeans": residents of the region surrounding Jerusalem at the time of Jesus' death who were gathered together for the festival of Passover. But why would the disciples be afraid of the Judeans? It was, after all, the Romans who killed Jesus. Pilate may have protested Jesus' innocence, but if you listen carefully to the text you can see that Pilate is just playing with the crowd, taunting them: "If you want this man to be put to death, kill him yourselves"—all the while knowing full well that he, Pilate, is the only one with the authority to carry out that act.[1] Ultimately, John places in the mouths of the Judeans the words that Pilate is waiting to hear: "If you release this man, you are no friend of the emperor" (John 19:12), followed a few verses later by the declaration, "We have no king but the emperor" (John 19:15).

Fear at work. The Judeans see the edge of the cliff looming: they know that they must demonstrate their loyalty to the emperor or face death themselves. It is a fear we also know in our own various contexts, not only those who are members of LGBTQ communities but also those who live in fear of us. And it is a fear that is real. Many of those for whom the Gospel of John was written, sometime in the latter part of the first century, would have seen the charred remains of Jerusalem, destroyed by the Romans in 70 CE, and the smell would still be burning in their nostrils.

Sitting behind closed doors, the disciples believe themselves to be poised on the edge of a cliff. They have seen the violence of the world up close and they know the power of fear to turn a crowd into a mob. The door, shut and barred, gives them the illusion that they are protected from

1. See Carter, *John and Empire*, 289–314.

the world. But with the same action that has locked the world out, they have also locked themselves in. If they sit behind the door long enough, the sweat of their fear will cause them to smell much like the body of Lazarus after it had been in the tomb for four days.

Just as Jesus came to the tomb of Lazarus, whom he loved, John says that Jesus came to the tomb that the disciples had created for themselves and, standing in their midst, greeted them with the words, "Peace be with you" (John 20:19).

This is not the first time Jesus has spoken words of peace to the disciples. Before his death, Jesus had told them, "Peace I leave with you; my peace I give to you. I do not give to you as the world gives. Do not let your hearts be troubled, and do not let them be afraid" (John 14:27). And yet here they are, afraid. It is one thing to hear such words before trouble begins; it is another to try to hold onto them when trouble is on your doorstep. As reassuring as Jesus' words may have been to the disciples, they point to a certain irony in this scene: how can you experience peace when you are living in fear?

There is no reaction on the part of the disciples until Jesus shows them the marks on his hands and his side. Then, John says, they rejoiced, for the one who was crucified now stands before them, fully alive. Yet this Jesus is not wholly the same Jesus they had known before; this Jesus bears the scars of crucifixion. He is a Jesus who has suffered at the hands of people driven by fear and, consequently, he is a Jesus who brings the disciples face to face with their own fears. Risen though he is, he offers them no false promises, and he certainly offers them no escape.

But he does offer them peace. His crucified presence reminds them that the peace he offers is not an easy peace; it is not a peace that will protect them like a shield from all potential harm. It is a peace that acknowledges fear, but refuses to let fear have the final word. It is a peace that, in the face of all that threatens to destroy life, continues to witness in tangible ways to the life-giving presence of God coming into the world. It is this peace to which the disciples are called to become a living witness in the world. But such a witness will be impossible so long as the disciples sit behind closed doors.

After showing them his hands and his side, Jesus once again says to the disciples, "Peace be with you. As [God] has sent me, so I send you" (John 20:21). "*As God has sent me, so I send you.*" Have you ever noticed that it is only in the Gospel of John that we are told that Jesus was sent? In the other Gospels he is born, baptized, led into the wilderness, but in John he is none of these things. He is, instead, sent—from God, into the world, because, we are told, God so loves the world. And Jesus tells the disciples that in the very same way that he was sent into the world, we too are sent—because of God's love for the world.

It's at this point that the real significance of the closed door becomes clear. In a letter written by a member of John's community the question is asked, "How does God's love abide in anyone who has the world's goods and sees a brother or sister in need and yet refuses help?" (1 John 3:17). The phrase "yet refuses help" masks a connection with the closed door. A more literal rendering of the verse from 1 John reads, "Whoever has what they need to live and sees a brother or sister in need but *closes the door* of their compassion against them, how does the love of God abide with them?" (In Greek, the connection is hard to miss because these are the only two places where John uses the verb meaning "to close or shut.") What 1 John reveals is that the moment the disciples close the door on the world because of fear, they also close the door on their compassion.

Now, it is important to acknowledge that when the writer of 1 John speaks of a brother or sister in need, he means a member of the community of faith—not the world. But I do not think that this fundamentally changes the issue, because the effect is the same: when we live in fear we construct walls to protect ourselves, and our goal becomes self-preservation.

There are times when this may be an appropriate response, when self-protection must be our first priority. Yet I believe that the wounds borne by the resurrected Jesus challenge us to evaluate in every situation whether or not we are simply using fear as an excuse to avoid the world and, in avoiding the world, to avoid facing what may prove to be the all too shallow depths of our compassion.

Those of us who identify as members of LGBTQ communities can come up with plenty of reasons to create walls in order to shut the rest of the world out. For many of us, fear has been a way of life—beginning with the first childhood taunt and continuing into adulthood, to the job we were told we could have as long as we, you know, kept it quiet. Walls have become a protective layer, one that shields our hearts, so that we hardly even notice their power over us anymore.

Meanwhile, much of the rest of the world has been busy building walls to shut us out. And every time an attempt has been made by good people to take the wall down, another wall has been constructed, reenforced and twice as thick, in an effort to create a space in which we don't even exist. Too many times, those walls have been constructed by those who baptized us, and confirmed us, and welcomed us into the church, only to usher us out again or to allow us to stay so long as, you know, we kept it quiet.

But there is a cost, in all of this, for everyone. When, driven by fear, we lock others out—and ourselves in—our capacity for compassion withers to fit the size of the too small space that we now inhabit. And we may begin to believe that Jesus, whose presence can be neither locked in nor locked out, is to be found only in the fearful tomb that we have created.

The writer of 1 John goes on to say, "There is no fear in love, but perfect love casts out fear" (1 John 4:18). "Perfect" does not mean without flaw. It means love that is mature: that is, love that is not driven by fashion or dependent on the thin ice of emotion. It is love that is grounded in a deep sense of commitment, love that does not turn when confronted by fear but sets aside fear in order to be present to those in need. It is this love that brought Jesus to the tomb of Lazarus, although he knew danger awaited him there, and it is this love that brings Jesus to the room where the disciples have entombed themselves. It is this love, also, that invites the disciples—invites us—to face our fear, to roll back the door of our tomb, and to become a sign of the life-giving presence of God coming into the world.

But the door isn't open yet. Back behind closed doors with the disciples, Jesus goes on to speak words that are frightening in the power they seem to place in the hands of the disciples. Most translations render the words of Jesus this way: "If you forgive the sins of any, they are forgiven; if you retain the sins of any, they are retained." Oddly enough, this is the *only* place in the entire Gospel of John where the words *forgive* and *forgiveness* occur. Why does the writer of the Gospel wait to talk about forgiveness until this point in the story, at the very end of the Gospel and behind closed doors? The answer lies in translation and context.

The translation of this verse poses a puzzle. "If you forgive the sins of any, they are forgiven" is clear enough, but what about the words that follow: "if you retain the sins of any, they are retained"? In fact, the word *sin* is an addition in English. A more literal translation of this final phrase is this: "If you grab hold of any, they are held fast." It is still possible to hear this as a reference to sins, that is, "If you grab hold of the sins of any, they are held fast." Yet read this way, the verse seems to say more about us than about the other person. It suggests that we have grabbed so tightly onto something we identify as sin in another person that we cannot let go. Whether driven by anger, or fear, or resentment, we have established a kind of death grip and thrown away the key. And as a result, we are then both held fast.

Yet there is another way to translate this verse: "Whose sins you shall forgive they are forgiven to them and those [meaning the *people* whose sins have been forgiven] whom you embrace are held fast."[2] Translated this way, the second phrase instructs us to embrace those whose sins have been forgiven and to hold them fast. Thus in the same way that Jesus declares, "This is the will of the One who sent me, that I should lose nothing of all that God has given me" (John 6:39), so too the community of faith is instructed to hold fast to those who have been given to them.[3] This too says as much about us as it does about the other person. If we receive the baptized into our communities of faith, we are called to embrace them and hold them dear.

Whichever way we hear these words, it is important to hear them in context. Jesus is speaking these words to the disciples, the gathered community, who are sitting behind closed doors, in fear. If forgiveness is needed anywhere, it strikes me that it is here, within the community of the baptized. Because when we are afraid we begin to point fingers at each other, and call each other names, and shun one another, and forget that those around us are the very ones whom God has entrusted to us.

And if there is anywhere that we need to hold each other in dear embrace, it is here as well: in the midst of our fear, even when our fears may be for very different reasons. For it is just possible that, as we embrace one another, we may discover that love prevails over fear. And in this discovery, we may find the courage to unlock the door.

Behind closed doors, Jesus does one more thing: he breathes on the disciples, saying, "Receive the Holy Spirit" (John 20:22). With this breath of new life, Jesus evokes the words spoken by the prophet Ezekiel: "Thus says the Lord GOD: Come from the four winds, O breath, and breathe upon these slain, that they may live" (Ezek 37:9). Into their self-created tomb, where the disciples sit, slain by fear, God once more sends God's Spirit to breathe new life into those who teeter on the edge between life and death.

This same Spirit of life comes to us in our own entombed spaces. It is a sign of God's love coming into the world. And it is a love that, bearing the marks of crucifixion, invites us to set aside our fear, to hold fast to one another, to roll back the stone and to hear God's voice calling to us, saying,

2. This translation is proposed in Schneiders, *Jesus Risen in Our Midst*, 146.
3. Ibid., 147.

"Come forth." Because we are loved by God. And because God loves the world.

Therefore, let us unbind ourselves from our shrouds of fear, take one another by the hand, and together bravely enter the world into which we have been sent.

# 25

# Why I Changed My Mind on Homosexuality

## Danny Cortez

The Reverend Danny Cortez, an ordained minister in the Southern Baptist Convention, is the pastor of New Heart Community Church, a Southern Baptist congregation in La Mirada, California. This sermon was preached at New Heart on February 9, 2014, just a few weeks after Rev. Cortez informed the elders that his views on homosexuality had changed. The congregation then entered a period of discernment, and on May 18, 2014, voted not to dismiss Rev. Cortez. Instead, they chose to become a "third way" church, leaving room for congregants to disagree with one another regarding the affirmation of LGBTQ people—which is a significant step for a Southern Baptist church. Later that year, on September 23, the Southern Baptist Convention voted to break ties with New Heart Community Church. [Editor's note: This is an edited transcript that closely follows the audio file of this sermon. Slight modifications have been made to make it read more like a manuscript than a transcript.][1]

---

## Romans 1

I've been so grateful in the sixteen years of New Heart that we've never had a church split. We've never had any major crisis. We've never had any huge

[1]. You may view this sermon online by visiting http://www.youtube.com/watch?v=WqYvkVqVLFo. For more information on evangelical churches and "third way" approaches, see Wilson, *A Letter to My Congregation*.

146

ordeals that created major chaos. But, unfortunately, we are now embarking on our first one.

Many of you received an email asking you to attend today. The subject matter was about homosexuality—some of you know why, and some of you don't. The reason there is chaos right now is that I recently revealed to the elders that I have changed my stance on homosexuality. It was understood that this was a radical shift from the longstanding belief of our church. This was a radical shift from our statement of faith aligned with the Southern Baptist Convention. In the news that I delivered to the elders, I realized that I had dropped a bomb on them. I'm saddened that I created that confusion. They expressed to me that they wished I had shared this with them earlier on in the process, as I was going through this shift. In retrospect, I realize that I did them wrong by not sharing this with them sooner, and that I had done the church wrong.

But the fact remains that I've been on this journey, and my thinking on this matter has changed. There are implications for that; there are strong implications. I realize that it's grounds for termination. I realize that this might be my last message—I get that. But I'm also grateful that the elders have extended graciousness to me. Even in our strong disagreement, I want everyone to know there has been nothing but respect for one another. There's been a genuine sense of struggle and disagreement—and yet there's been love between us. And that's really all I can ask.

They have set a course of action for our church to pursue. The church will get together for the next few weeks to be in a time of discussion, dialogue, and prayer. I know this topic is often a litmus test for Christianity and liberalism versus conservatism. I know this is often the thing that makes people say, "Oh, you've become a flaming liberal! You've lost the faith!" I understand that, but I please ask of you that we would all create space right now to listen, to pay attention, to allow all of our hearts to be formed, and that I myself would be taught by you. Because I confess that on this journey, I don't have all of the theology down. My conclusions aren't tightly knit. I have so much room to grow, to be taught by you, to be taught by God. And I pray that all of our postures are the same. This is a difficult time.

Let me begin by telling you a little bit about my background. In my formative years of my faith, in high school, I attended Calvary Chapel. Then, in college, I became heavily involved with Campus Crusade for Christ (for the next twelve years). I also attended the Christian Missionary Alliance Church during college and was one of the youth leaders there. I also attended Biola University, Talbot Seminary, to pursue my master's

## Part Four: Calling for Transformation

degree in pastoral ministry. In 1993, I was ordained in the Southern Baptist denomination, and since that time, for the past twenty-one years, I have been an ordained Southern Baptist minister, the last sixteen years here at New Heart.

I say all of that to show you that my spiritual upbringing has been in conservative Christianity. It's been traditional in my bent toward theology and biblical interpretation. At the same time, I realize that my heart for the marginalized has continued to grow.

Sixteen years ago when New Heart started, I remember the first time someone came up to me and asked, "Danny, can I meet with you?" There was an individual who confessed to me their same-sex attraction. I remember not knowing what to do. I was caught off-guard and prayed for them. And lo and behold, for the next sixteen years—every year—one or two or three people would come to me and tell me about their same-sex struggles. This pretty much became a pattern at New Heart.

One of the things that became clear to me as I began engaging in multiple discussions with people within the church—just trying to figure out and working through the anguish and the confusion they had—was that it always felt different from my interactions with everyone else inside the church and outside the church. Whenever I met with people with different problems—whether it be drug addiction or pornography or their spiritual walk or adultery or committing some kind of crime—I could sit with them, engaged, and deliver God's word. And I always felt like I was giving them life. I always felt like, "Stay close to God, and follow these commandments of Christ." And it was always received with, "Yes, I know. That's good; that feels right. It's hard, but it feels right."

But whenever I met with someone who had same-sex identity issues, I would sit down with them and they would say, "Danny, what do you think about this?" I would tell them, "The Bible is clear. God is against homosexual behavior. And because of that, you have to remain celibate."

In these dialogues, there was a sense of dread that would suddenly come upon the people I would talk to. It was basically me telling them, "For the rest of your life, you can never fall in love. For the rest of your life, you should never give yourself or anybody permission to love you in an intimate manner." Those kinds of words—when I said those words—I could just feel the dread coming into the person I was talking to. I was always wondering why . . . of all God's commandments, why is this the one commandment that just seemed like it was different from all of the other commandments that seemed to impart life? This was the one that created so much self-hatred. It made people feel like they were imprisoned—serving a sentence of life with no chance to love. Matthew Vines puts it this way:

> Good teachings, even when they are very difficult, are not destructive to human dignity. They don't lead to emotional and spiritual devastation, and to the loss of self-esteem and self-worth. But those have been the consequences for gay people of the traditional teaching on homosexuality. It has not borne good fruit in their lives, and it's caused them incalculable pain and suffering. If we're taking Jesus seriously that bad fruit cannot come from a good tree, then that should cause us to question whether the traditional teaching is correct.[2]

I remember one encounter I had with a young lesbian girl who used to attend our church. She was in dialogue with me, saying, "Danny, are you sure you know what the Bible is saying?" We started talking about reparative therapy and what some people were pushing her towards, those who were trying to get her to change her sexual orientation. I'll never forget what she told me that day at the coffee shop. She said, "Danny, will you look at that man who's sitting at the next table over? How would you feel if I told you that you had to somehow go over there and hold his hand? How would you feel if I told you that you had to kiss him? That you had to fall in love with him? That you had to learn how to be intimate with him?"

I remember looking over there, and I experienced a knee-jerk reaction because I'm straight. She said, "Danny, this is how I feel whenever I hear the church telling me, 'If you don't want to be celibate, this is the only option for you.' Danny, do you understand how dehumanizing that feels? Do you understand how gross it makes me feel? In the same way right now—you reacted that way—that's how I react. That's why it's so hard for me to understand why God would confine someone to this lifelong confusion and loneliness and imprisonment to celibacy."

After she left New Heart, she said, "Danny, I know you've been thinking about studying this topic for a long time now." She knew that I had a lot of topics that I was rethinking, and homosexuality was toward the bottom of the list. She said, "Danny, I pray that you would finally put this at the top of your list." Three years ago, she left, and I said, "I will. I'll do that."

And I realized toward the beginning of this more intensified and intentional study that I had to admit that much of what I knew about

2. Vines, "The Gay Debate."

Part Four: Calling for Transformation

homosexuality was not the result of a long period of study, but it was something that was passed down to me by either my parents or the church. I just never took the time to actually challenge any of those thoughts, but I was now at a place where I realized I had to engage in it.

As I began my study, I realized there were only six passages in all of Scripture that really were directly associated with homosexuality. Three of them are in the New Testament. Three of them are in the Old. And there's not a lot of time this morning to go through all of them, so I want to focus on the main one, and that's Romans 1.

Here, Paul is writing this most epic of epistles. Keep in mind, he's trying to write about the glory of God and justification by faith and how grace abounds and how all of us have fallen short of the glory of God. He's writing about these great truths, and like any good writer, he's trying to come up with a great introduction. So what Paul does in the very beginning, in Romans 1, is write,

> Although they claim to be wise, they became fools and exchanged the glory of the immortal God for images made to look like a mortal human being and birds and animals and reptiles. Therefore God gave them over in the sinful desires of their hearts to sexual impurity for the degrading of their bodies with one another. They exchanged the truth of God for a lie, and worshiped the created things rather than the Creator—who is forever praised. Amen. Because of this, God gave them over to shameful lusts. Even their women exchanged natural sexual relations for unnatural ones. In the same way the men abandoned the natural relationships with women and were inflamed with lust for one another. Men committed shameful acts with other men, and received in themselves the due penalty for their error. . . . They are full of envy, murder, strife, deceit and malice. They are gossips, slanderers, God-haters, insolent, arrogant and boastful; they invent new ways of doing evil. Disobedient to parents, no understanding, no fidelity, no love, no mercy. Although they know God's righteous decree, that those who do such things deserve death, they not only continue to do these things but also approve of those who practice them. (Rom 1:22-32 NIV)

Paul is listing here the result of exchanging the truth of God for a lie. He's telling his audience, in effect, "You've exchanged God's truth for a lie and exchanged his glory. Now you're creating images made in the form of human beings and birds and animals and reptiles. You're worshiping these idols. Not only that, because of that idolatry, God hands you over. You're involved in this gross, sexual immorality. Men lying with men. Women committing unnatural relations. Then there's gossips, slanderers, God-haters. All of that."

As Paul is writing down this escalating crescendo of human sin and arrogance and evil, the listeners, the recipients of this letter, are tracking with Paul, and they're saying to Paul, "Yes, that's evil! That's right! Everything about what you're saying, we agree with!"

What Paul is doing, I think, is naming what everybody in the Christian circle at Rome (both Gentile and Jew) agree on—this problem in the temple at Rome. There was homosexual prostitution, violence, abuse, and all kinds of sexual immorality going on. Paul is setting up his letter, trying to name the most evil thing he can think of. And this is it. It's the evil Roman Empire, especially the practices of its leaders and the immorality that occurs within the temple. Everyone is saying, "Yes! Yes, that is evil!" And Paul has them in his hands now.

Just as the people are resonating with Paul and pointing fingers, saying, "That is so despicable!," in the very first verse of Romans 2 Paul turn the tables on his audience. He writes, "You, therefore, have no excuse, you who pass judgment on someone else, for at whatever point you judge another, you are condemning yourself, because you who pass judgment do the same things" (Rom 2:1 NIV). Paul is saying, "The reason I wrote what I wrote in Romans 1 was to create a realization of how great *your* sin is." In his magnificent, brilliant writing style, Paul gets his readers to agree with how evil all of this is but then tells them, "Guess what? You're just the same way!" Therefore, Paul says, don't judge anyone.

And yet, Romans 1 is the passage used most often to judge all sorts of people, especially those in the LGBTQ community. So, if I were to look at Paul's intent in Romans 1, it's not as a window into other people's lives. Rather, it's a mirror to look at my own life. It's not a window where we're supposed to be looking at homosexuality and other people with disgust. In the application that I read here—really the only clear application that Paul is giving in this extended passage—the reason he writes this is for us to understand our own sinfulness. So that we can understand our own need for God; so that we can understand our solidarity with humanity.

I think Paul is brilliant in the way he did it. It's the New Testament equivalent of what the prophet Nathan did to King David in 2 Samuel after David committed adultery, taking someone else's wife. Nathan tells David a parable about a rich man who stole a poor man's only lamb and killed it. David hears the parable and says, "That man must be killed." Nathan says, "Guess what, David? That man is you." The purpose of the parable was to show David his own sinfulness.[3] And that's the purpose of Romans 1.

But I know for many of us, that's not enough. Yes, maybe that's the purpose of Romans 1, but it still doesn't excuse the fact that Paul is declaring that these things are still sinful. I get that. But I think part of the problem here in reading Romans 1—in regard to the homosexual passages—is that it's very natural for us to read it with Western eyes, from our own cultural context. We have to understand that Romans was written in the context of their own particular history.

Let me give you an example. If, one day, I were to preach a sermon on the depravity of modern America, and I said, "In our society, men take advantage of interns, and they have sex with them. They not only take advantage of interns and have sex with them, but when they're confronted by that evil, they deny it, and they wag their fingers, and they say, 'I did not sleep with that woman!'" All of you would understand what I'm talking about without me even having to say the names of the president and the intern I'm referring to.

But imagine if somebody two thousand years from now heard a podcast and said, "Hey, that teaching must mean that men shouldn't have sex with interns." That's what happens when we lose the historical context of what's going on.

So the question for me is, "What is happening politically around the time of Paul?" Is there something in that cultural context that was actually feeding a common story that everybody could automatically agree with and say, "Hey, Paul. I'm tracking with you, and we all know who you're talking about." And I think that's what's happening because there's a person within history that nearly fits this Romans 1 passage to a T.

I want to read excerpts from James Brownson's book *Bible, Gender, Sexuality*. I pray that you would track with me on this. The portion I'm reading is a little lengthy.

> Neil Elliott has called attention to the striking similarities between Paul's language and the incredible greed, violence, and sexual excesses of Gaius Caligula, an emperor who reigned in a period not too long before Paul wrote Romans. First of all, Gaius is closely linked to the practice of idolatry. The Roman writer Suetonius

---

3. See 2 Sam 12:1–13.

reports how Gaius "set up a special temple to his own godhead, with priests and with victims of the choicest kind." Another Roman writer, Dio Cassius, comments negatively on how Gaius was the only emperor to claim to be divine and to be the recipient of worship during his lifetime. Gaius also tried at one point to erect a statue of himself in the Temple of Jerusalem.[4]

That's why the Jews despised this guy. Here's a guy that was kind of defacing their own temple. "[H]e was dissuaded only by a delegation from Herod—hence the link between Gaius and idolatry would have been well-known indeed, particularly in Jewish circles."[5] Brownson continues:

> Gaius also serves as "Exhibit A" for out-of-control lust. Suetonius reports how Gaius "lived in perpetual incest with all his sisters, and at a large banquet he placed each of them in turn below him, while his wife reclined above." He records gruesome examples of Gaius's arbitrary violence, vindictiveness, and cruelty. Later, Suetonius chronicles Gaius's sexual liaisons with the wives of dinner guests, raping them in an adjoining room and then returning to the banquet to comment on their performance. Various same-sex sexual encounters between Gaius and other men are similarly recounted. Finally, a military officer whom he had sexually humiliated joined a conspiracy to murder him, which they did less than four years into his reign. Suetonius records that Gaius was stabbed through the genitals when he was murdered. One wonders whether we can hear an echo of this gruesome story in Paul's comments in Romans 1:27: "Men committed shameless acts with men and received in their own person the due penalty for their error." Gaius Caligula graphically illustrates the reality of which Paul speaks in Romans 1: the movement from idolatry to every insatiable lust, to every form of depravity and the violent, murderous reprisal. . . . [The Jewish writer] Philo writes in similarly scathing terms of the evils of Gaius Caligula, interpreting his depravity as the result of his refusal to honor God, and his death as a manifestation of divine justice. This suggests that Gaius's excesses and the divine judgment incurred by them were a common theme that would have been familiar to many Jews in the ancient world.
>
> These contemporary parallels . . . give a clearer sense of the kinds of linkages and associations that Paul's readers would have made as they read his words in Romans 1. Paul is speaking of sinfulness in its extreme and most obvious forms here. His goal

---

4. Brownson, *Bible, Gender, Sexuality*, 156–57.
5. Ibid., 157.

is to clearly delineate the essence of the human problem and to secure the unambiguous agreement of the Roman Christians in condemning such outrageousness.... The twenty-one vices recounted in Romans 1:29–31 recount the full depth and breadth of human corruption, the sort of outrageous conduct that could be seen in Gaius Caligula.[6]

The readers of Romans 1, who were very well aware of this evil Roman ruler, would read this passage and think, "We know who you're talking about. We know that this is about the excesses. It's not just homosexual behavior, but it's the violence of the homoerotic behavior that is occurring in that evil Roman ruler and everyone around him."

That's why I think it's so important for us to not make the mistake of reading Romans 1 and then saying, "Isn't it clear? Isn't it clear that God says this?" When, in actuality, the context of the history says so much more.

I wish I had more time to go through the other two Bible passages in the New Testament, 1 Cor 6:9 and 1 Tim 1:10, where it speaks about homosexuality in a list of sins. The Greek word that is being translated is *arsenokoitēs*. And if you know anything about that word, you know that it is a very hard word to translate. In fact, it wasn't until 1950 that the word *homosexual* was in any English Bible. Before 1950, the word *homosexual* wasn't even in any of the translations because, partly, *homosexual* is a new word. It was coined in the 1800s. So, I grant that *arsenokoitēs* might refer to "homosexuality." There's definitely an argument to be stated that it could mean that. But it could also mean "sexual immorality." It could also mean "sexual perversion." In fact, there's such little usage of it in antiquity that people agree that Paul was probably the first person to coin this word.

The New Testament scholar Gordon Fee—if you've ever been to seminary, you know who this guy is—he says, "*Arsenokoitēs* is rarely used in the Greek literature, especially when describing homosexual activity."[7] So here's this New Testament scholar saying that this word is hard to figure out because it's used in so many different ways.

Then you look at Martin Luther's version of the Bible when he translated into German the words of Paul and his letters. He translated it as "boy abusers." He saw *arsenokoitēs* as pedophilia. If you trace this word throughout history, you'll realize there's a wide spectrum of use, which has created doubt that anyone really knows for sure what the word means. Should we

---

6. Ibid., 157–58.
7. Fee, *First Epistle to the Corinthians*, 244.

translate it as "homosexual"? Well, that's what [some of] our modern versions have chosen. But I'm not so convinced.

When I think of Middle Eastern sexual practices, I realize I'm not an authority in them. In fact, whenever I think about the Middle East and see pictures and videos of it, I'm always thinking, "Wow, that's a different place." Whenever they sing their songs, or shout in the streets, I don't get it. I know there's a reason for all of that, but I don't understand it.

Then I think, "How much more do I not understand Middle Eastern marriage and sexual practices? That must be even more different than I can comprehend." Then I think, "How much more difficult is it to understand Middle Eastern sexual practices from two thousand, three thousand years ago?"

I knew if I was going to do a serious study of this, I had to immerse myself in what was going on. I couldn't just read about it and look at the scholarly research on it. I needed to get ahold of homoerotic literature, and that's what I did. I tried to grab every piece of homoerotic literature that has ever been written in the Roman and Greek periods. And I began to immerse myself, all in order to better understand.

There were times when my body just shook with disgust. There were so many times I read it, and I was like, "Are you kidding me?" I felt like I was being transported into this otherworldly reality that was just so bizarre and evil and disgusting and misogynistic. So brutally violent, where these old men would just treat young boys like they were nothing. I kept reading it over and over, and I thought, "You know what? That's a different world. That's a different world."

This is why, if you ever read classical historians today, who research homoerotic literature and teach at the universities and write the books, they'll all say in unison, "It's really hard to talk about homosexuality, because our idea of homosexuality is so different from what it was back then." There's always this thing in the beginning of the book that is asking us to try to think of this in a way that is very different [from what we understand].

One of the ways that it's different is that in our Western context, we tend to think of the dichotomy of homosexual versus heterosexual. But they didn't think in those ways back then. They didn't think, "Well, here are the straight people, and here are the homosexuals." The way they thought was in terms of active versus passive, or dominant versus submissive, or masculine versus feminine. In other words, in homoerotic behavior, there's a dominant, and there's a passive. The dominant was usually older, or a free person. The passive was sometimes a young boy, a slave. The way this worked was the dominant would penetrate the passive, but it would never be reversed. Just that alone makes you realize that the type of homosexual behavior that was occurring back in antiquity was so different from what's happening now. What was filled with violence and abuse, I look at, and I think about all the things I read, and I say, "Hey, God, you were right to condemn all of that. God, that was wicked! All of that stuff! That's unjust! God, I believe your word; no one should behave that way."

But as you begin to realize that we've moved away from that part of history, we find something very different.

It's almost like Halloween. I remember when our kids were first born, I was thinking, "Should I let my kids do Halloween?" Because I remember watching a Calvary Chapel video that said it's demonic. You go trick-or-treating, and you're actually worshiping Satan, and blah blah blah blah. Then I realized, "No, I don't think they're really doing that, so let's go trick-or-treating!"

But if you look at the origins of it, it's true. It was cultic. They would build bonfires, sacrifice animals, wear costumes, go trick-or-treating, and receive food in return for prayers for the dead. So, in terms of Halloween, I could make a case that no one should do Halloween because of its origins, which are filled with cultic practices. But we know that it's okay to do Halloween now. Why? Because the meaning has changed.

And that's what I feel like has happened. Homosexual behavior is not what it was in biblical days, when it was filled with violence and abuse and rape and slavery and temple prostitution. When I go into that world and have to put down the book, and I meet with a lesbian couple who are friends of mine at Starbucks, I think, "What I just came from in my book doesn't feel like this at all. Because here's a lesbian Christian couple meeting me for coffee, and they're praying for me. They're sharing the words of Christ with me. They're loving on me." And I'm like, "This is not what I'm reading about. This is different. This is different."

I know that someone will probably pick up this podcast and write a refutation of everything I've said. I've been following this debate for long enough now. One scholar puts out something, another will put out something, then they'll put out something else.

And it just keeps going. And I've been following it, and I've been realizing that for every response, there's an answer, and for every answer, there's a response. And it just keeps escalating. Quite frankly, my head is hurting just trying to follow the discussion.

Then I think, "Here I am, someone who is seminary-trained, who has learned Hebrew and Greek. I'm tracking with this, I'm tracking with this. But what about the rest of the people who don't have time for this? How are they ever going to come to their own conclusions? Do you really have to be a scholar to try to determine what the will of God is? Is truth only reserved for those who are debating in scholarly research? And then the way we arrive at it is by faith? All of us have to align ourselves with someone we think is more respectable and smarter? So we align ourselves that way, by faith? 'I think I'm just going to go with him.'"

Really, that's how the blogs have been. Or is there a different way? Because I don't think Jesus intended his truth to be revealed only to the learned, but to the simple. And Jesus says, "You look at a fruit, is it bad, or is it good? Because a good tree bears good fruit. A bad tree bears bad fruit."[8] And everybody knows we're wired to recognize hatred. We're wired to recognize injustice. We're wired to recognize things that are evil.

So we don't have to have all that knowledge and then jump by faith, to lean on one scholar. I pray that none of you would look at me and say, "Hey, I'm with Pastor Danny," because I'm fallible myself. I'm still in process. What God says to you, as people of faith, is, "Look at the fruit." And what I see in my conversations with the homosexual community—I see the homosexual community being marginalized over and over and over again by the church. I say something's wrong with that picture. Why is it that in our churches, it's almost like there's a sign outside of our doors that says, "No Homosexuals Allowed"? Or at our communion tables, "Are you straight? Only straight people here." Really, that's what goes on, and people in the LGBTQ community, they're feeling like the churches don't accept them.

Of course, what will be said is, "We have to guard the purity of the church. We have to remain strong. We have to look at God's word and not compromise."

Then I think about Jesus, who was the most morally pure person I can ever think of. He didn't create walls of separation. He didn't do that. What he did was he went to their homes. He went to their frickin' homes. And when a prostitute came in, a girl who was an abomination and dirty—and no priest would want to be seen next to her—what does she do? She washes Jesus' feet with her tears, with her hair. Then he tells these scholars, these

---

8. See Matt 7:18.

## Part Four: Calling for Transformation

theologians, these pastors, "You study the Scriptures. In them, you think you have eternal life. You go around following all these rabbis. You can debate all you want. But do you want to know what true worship is? It's not about debate and trying to figure out the Torah. It's by watching someone like this girl who has been marginalized. If you want to know worship, you learn it through this person."[9]

If you want to know what giving is, you don't buy a book on giving. You look at the widow who had nothing. If you want to know what love looks like, you don't buy a book about love. You look at the Samaritan who was considered faulty of theology, a compromiser by virtue of his identity. You look at someone who's been marginalized, and you see that this is how to love.[10]

That's what I've been doing. I've been going into the homosexual community, into the LGBTQ areas. I've been going to AIDS clinics. I've been going to gay bars. I've been going to gay coffeehouses, bringing my books, studying, trying to meet people. I've been going to gay conferences, listening to their stories, letting them vent to me the abuse they have felt from the church. And there I am, listening, and saying, "I'm sorry. I am so sorry." Within those conversations, I realized that in those places, I saw the presence of God.

Over the summer, I remember thinking, "Wow, did I just change my view?" I remember it was just a thought in my mind, and it caught me off-guard. "Do I now believe that same-sex marriage and relationships in a loving, monogamous way is permitted by Scripture?" And I remember thinking, "Whoa, that felt weird. Did I just become liberal? Did I just lose my faith?" I remember I was scared about that, actually. I didn't intend to do that.

Then I heard a song on the radio, and I thought, "Oh my gosh, that's a pro-gay song, and I'm actually liking it." I thought, "Oh, man. What's wrong with me?" And I remember not wanting to talk it over with anybody until one day when I was driving my son, Drew, to school. That song came on the radio again, and I was like, "Oh, here's that song!" I looked over at Drew, and I said, "Hey, Drew. Who sings this?"

Drew said, "It's Macklemore. How come, Dad?"

I said, "Oh, because I like this song."

---

9. See Luke 7:36–50.
10. See Mark 12:41–44 and Luke 10:25–37, respectively.

Drew looked over and said, "Dad, you like this song? Do you know what this is about?"

I said, "Yeah, I know what it's about. I think I changed my thoughts about homosexuality."

He remained silent. I could tell that he felt a little confused. As we got out of the car—I was helping him with something in school—I looked over at him, and I said, "Drew, what do you think about it?"

He turned to me, and he told me in a nervous voice, "Dad, I'm gay." I remember I just turned around, and I hugged him so hard. I said, "I love you so much, son. I love you so much. And I accept, and I affirm you. And I will love you unconditionally."

It was just the most meaningful moment that I had ever had with Drew. I felt like I had lost so many years of not knowing the pain that was going on in his heart and thinking, "Drew, why didn't you tell me before?"

He said, "Dad, if I said anything, I would be admitting that I was giving up. I was trying to fight my gayness. I didn't want to admit it, and I hated myself. I hated myself all the time."

I said, "Drew, I'm so sorry for not being there with you. But know that I will be your father, and I will love you. I will love you unconditionally."

I couldn't help thanking God. Drew was born two months after New Heart started, and the whole time of New Heart was in preparation for this. It was in preparation for this moment. I said, "God, thank you. Thank you that you brought me to a place where I'm no longer judging people who think differently from me. God, how freeing that is."

As we caught up to my son's life, we felt like we had lost so much time with him. On his birthday, last December 30, he said to us, "You know, this is the first time I woke up on my birthday where I was at peace."

I said, "What do you mean?"

He said, "Every birthday, I would wake up and realize I'm still gay, and I knew God hadn't answered my prayer."

There was another time in the car when he said, "Dad, Mom, I want you to know that if somebody gave me a pill that could change my gayness, I would take it right now."

And so I thought about that. I went up to him the next day, and I said, "Drew, I want you to know that if I had a pill that could change you, I wouldn't give it to you, because you're perfect just the way you are. No more fighting, Drew. No more fighting. Accept the way God has made you. Because I love you just the way you are."

## Part Four: Calling for Transformation

For the first time, speaking to someone who was gay, I felt like I was giving them life. For the first time, I was actually offering words of life. I thought, "The fruit of this feels familiar. It feels so familiar." I might not have all my theology down, and there are some passages that I'm still working through, but I know what fruit looks like. I know what good fruit looks like. I might not have all the answers, and someone might be able to stump me with a question, so that I have to say, "I have no idea. I don't know. I'm just ignorant that way."

But I do know what grace and mercy and peace and love look like.

And so we see in the life of Jesus—the perfectly sinless man who was willing to cross over forty-five boundaries in Scripture—he crossed social, religious, and political boundaries in an effort to stand in solidarity with the other person. That, for me, has been what my journey is about. That's why I spend time talking with the elderly who have been abandoned. That's why, last week, I sat down with a rapist who had been in and out of jail. That's why I meet with brothel owners and prostitutes. That's why I sit down with the homeless and listen to their stories. Because, for me, the study of God and the way I find truth is no longer by trying to find the best arguments, the best books, the best scholarly research. It's looking at the way Jesus lived his life and finding the kingdom of God in the things that people deem worthless and the people who are most broken.

My hope for New Heart isn't that you all would agree with me. It's been a sixteen-year journey for me to finally get to where I am. I don't expect anyone to agree with what I believe. I'm not here trying to push my beliefs on you but merely to share with you my journey, and you have every right . . . I respect whatever you believe. But do we as a church have space for disagreement? Are we as a church willing to say that we have different ideas of homosexuality, and therefore, can we not judge anyone and just accept them into full membership? Or do we choose to say, "We disagree with you, and therefore, we have no fellowship with you"? Personally, I don't think that's the way of Christ. I don't think that's the way of Christ.

On January 8, my wife and I went to Chicago. Some of you follow us on Facebook. Many of you were asking, "Why in the world did you go to Chicago? It's so cold!" No one knew the real reason why we were going except our family. The reason Abby and I went to Chicago was to go to the Gay Christian Network Conference. I found out there was a conference in Chicago to help parents who needed a support group, and Abby and I qualified for that because we're so darned ignorant on how to raise a gay child. Somebody, please, teach me.

But it wasn't about raising him, actually. It was about raising ourselves. Erasing some of our biases. Our prejudices.

At this conference, there were over seven hundred people there—maybe sixty parents, and the rest people in the LGBTQ community. Here we were, sitting in a hotel conference room, singing the same songs we sing here at church. They were lifting their hands, and I was looking over at Abby, and I was wondering how she felt because she grew up Southern Baptist, all her life. Her grandfather was Southern Baptist, her uncle, her dad, her cousins. All those people are pastors in her family. I was wondering, "Dear, how do you feel?"

She was like, "It's different."

I remember thinking, "This is where Jesus would be. This is where Jesus would be."

The last night, I met a man by the name of Coyote. He approached me, thanking me for my story—I told some people about my journey. He said, "This conference is meaningful for me and my friends because this is the only church we get to go to—once a year."

I was like, "What do you mean?"

He said, "In the places we live, in the small communities, there are no churches that will accept us."

And my heart broke. I thought, "That really sucks."

So, when I was asked the question recently, "How does it feel to know that you might be terminated in a few weeks?" I said, "I am at peace." I'm at peace because I know my heart has been enlarged for people like Coyote who need a church. I know that whatever happens, compassion is giving me clarity. It's giving me clarity in my calling; it's giving me clarity in my purpose. People like Coyote, they need a church. They need to be pastored. They need a community of people who will not judge them because of their sexual identity.

So, I pray that as a church we would open ourselves to how God directs us, and I caution you to realize that it's so easy to look at the word of God and merely look at the letter of the law. But there is something underneath it, a deeper current, that is only understood by the Spirit, moved by love, and drawn into compassion. Our thoughts cannot just be about arguing the biblical text. It must be understood in the context of love, and that means in the context of real, human relationships. Because compassion is what gives clarity to this matter.

And I pray that our church would survive this.

## 26

## Picking Up the Mantle

RICHARD F. WARD

The Reverend Dr. Richard F. Ward is the Fred B. Craddock Professor of Homiletics and Worship (and Director of Denominational Formation for United Church of Christ students) at Phillips Theological Seminary in Tulsa, Oklahoma. He is the author of *Speaking from the Heart* and *Speaking of the Holy*. This sermon was preached as a keynote address for the Leadership Training School for the Christian Church Disciples of Christ (Oklahoma Region) at First Christian Church in Oklahoma City, Oklahoma, on February 2, 2013.

---

2 *Kings* 2:1–14

The king of Israel was dead.
The royal obituary read: "King Ahaziah died of complications from a fall from his roof."
The official memorial service probably didn't take very long.
The royal spin doctors must have had a hard time preparing his list of accomplishments.
On the throne for two years—he did put down that rebellion—but uh
He did fail to reach that trade agreement with the allies—
Another king—dead from a fall from a high place—how appropriate.

But the dynasty of the infamous Ahab and Jezebel would continue.
Jorem was on the throne—he sits in the story as a symbol
Of government that treats the humanity it serves as commodities
That is annoyed by questions of human worth
It's clear to Jorem—productivity establishes human worth

That view of government sounded all too familiar to the people of Israel
They knew their history
Israel was looking more and more like the place they escaped—Egypt
Ahab had looked a lot like Pharaoh and Jezebel his consort
Why, their sons Ahaziah and Jorem were spitting images!
The established civil religion promised fertility, security, and prosperity
For those who worshipped Baal—it was so popular that it had all but
Swallowed up the memory of God

The God who had delivered them once upon a time from Pharaoh
The God who hated tyranny—particularly among God's own people
Especially when that tyranny was built on the back of the working poor and helpless
Where was God now?
The God of Israel has been cast out of the royal court
But was waiting out in the wilderness
Waiting for a "school of prophets" to gather
The theme of the gathering is "leadership during a transitional time"
They are waiting for Elijah and Elisha to cross over into the wilderness

Why the wilderness?
Because the wilderness is one of God's favorite places
To fashion a community that will serve as God's partners in redemption
Because the wilderness is a place where memory comes alive
Where God's people discover not only God makes provision
But where God's people discover that they have what it takes to survive
And yes to flourish even in a place where resources appear to be scarce

Is it a surprise then that God is leading Elijah, Elisha, and a "school of the prophets" out into a wilderness during this time of political change?
One king is dead in the story, another has assumed the throne,

## Part Four: Calling for Transformation

but the ghosts of Pharaoh, of Ahab, and Jezebel are alive and well
Pharaoh's spirit is present whenever those in power want to form a government
That treats its people like annoyances if they do not produce
And tells us that's just the way it has to be.

God leads them out of the political world to turn on their prophetic imaginations
To take them—for a time—out of the political world to sharpen their vision
To open their ears to hear some hard lessons about power
In the political world addiction to power can overwhelm the desire to serve
In the Realm of God, God's Spirit empowers the desire to serve

God is leading them out to the wilderness
because God has a promise to fulfill to God's people
God will not leave God's people without leadership
In stressful times.

The wilderness in the Bible represents any place
Where God will take those who are called to be leaders, teachers, disciples
To train and retrain them for the hard work of fashioning and refashioning
A community of God's Covenant partners.

The wilderness could be a place—like this
How do we know when we are in the wilderness?
Because many of us are asking the same questions that wilderness people ask.
How are we going to survive?
We remember a time of abundance and prosperity.
What is it that will sustain us now?
What resources do we have that we can share?
Will we make it out of here? And if we do what will our community look like?

Wilderness people recognize that they are not close to centers of power

Where influence is peddled, where commodities are exchanged
Where decisions are made that affect the future
There are those who are close to those centers of power
Who are already writing drafts of our obituaries
"They didn't live like kings," they want to write,
"but they spoke and acted like they were in charge."
There was a time when there was royalty in the pulpit
But then something happened—they "fell" from the high place of esteem
But now find themselves on the margins of relevance
They used to be called "mainline"—but no more.

Wilderness people know that the wilderness is a place of testing our faith
Where we are tempted to believe those who would write our obituaries
That there is no longer a role for us to play in God's movement,
And if there is a God at all, God has sent messengers to relay the news to us
That there is no longer a place for us at the Table, no call for our opinion.

So if that were true, then why has God summoned us to this assembly this day?
Why is God using this ancient text to call us to this wilderness, here and now?
Perhaps it's because God sees us differently
than those who would write us off see us.
I believe we are gathered here today as a "school of prophets"
Who are assembled to consider issues of leadership
During a time of upheaval, transition, and change

Maybe you have trouble thinking of yourselves as a "school of prophets."
Maybe God hasn't spoken to you—not in wind, not in fire,
Or even in a still small voice—yet.
Perhaps you feel the prophet's burden but you have not yet received
A clear vision of the future of the institutional church that you serve.

Maybe I can help.

## Part Four: Calling for Transformation

Do you know what scholars tell us about the "school of the prophets"
That appears in this text?
That they found themselves on the margins of political and religious power
Because of what they had committed themselves to
Because of their vision of what God was up to in the world
You see, prophets sense that something isn't quite right with the status quo.
Prophets have a way of speaking about and on behalf of those who are suffering
Prophets refuse to believe that the present reality is all the reality there is
Prophets refuse to give in to despair and fashion a word of relentless hope
In the face of oppression and exploitation
They come together as a "school"—like the gathering here—for mutual support
To share their visions and their wisdom, to encourage one another

I believe that you are gathering at a time that is ripe with hope
Prophets maintain a healthy skepticism about the ability of any government
To get in line with what God is up to in the world
But there are signs—hints—of a turn toward common sense and compassion
A fragile rebirth of civility and baby steps toward cooperation
Who will be the leaders who will help us make that turn?
Who will help to midwife the rebirth of civility in our communities?
Who will beat the drums so that these baby steps
May become a long and steady march?

Our text tells us that Elisha would now be the one to lead.
Elijah had taught him everything he could but now he was passing from the scene.
Many of those who are responsible for our being here today
Meeting with this school of prophets—have passed from the scene.
Parents and pastors, teachers, friends, even adversaries are here no longer.
The Spirit of God drops a mantle at Elisha's feet in this story.

I wonder how long it took Elisha to pick it up?
Did he wonder if he was ready?
Did he wonder if he had enough time to prepare?
Had he paid close enough attention to what his mentor told him
During the time they had together?
Did he wonder if the same power that was so evident in the life
Of his mentor, his teacher, his counselor, his adversary
Would be present with him?

What did it cost him to pick it up?
He could no longer hide in the wings holding Elijah's coat.
He could no longer depend on Elijah to speak for him.
He could no longer expect Elijah to act if he was too afraid.
The people of God needed Elisha, not a dim copy of his former teacher.
They needed his vision, his voice, his presence, his interpretation
Not warmed over versions of his mentors.

Elijah's ministry was right for his time
Now Elisha faced a new situation;
he would have to craft his ministry to address it.
Elisha is our representative in this story.
His time of preparation, study, mentorship, experience
Left him with the ability that God's people needed most.
The ability to see the reality of God's activity in the world
Even when that world was blinded by
The smoke screens of the Pharaohs among us.

The story drops a mantle at our feet.
How long will it take *us* to pick it up?

# For Further Reading

Lee, Justin. *Torn: Rescuing the Gospel from the Gays-vs.-Christians Debate.* New York: Jericho, 2012.
Rogers, Jack. *Jesus, the Bible, and Homosexuality: Explode the Myths, Heal the Church.* Rev. ed. Louisville: Westminster John Knox, 2009.
Spellers, Stephanie. *Radical Welcome: Embracing God, The Other, and the Spirit of Transformation.* New York: Church Publishing, 2006.
Vines, Matthew. *God and the Gay Christian: The Biblical Case in Support of Same-Sex Relationships.* Colorado Springs: Convergent, 2014.
Waun, Maurine. *More than Welcome: Learning to Embrace Gay, Lesbian, Bisexual, and Transgendered Persons in the Church.* St. Louis: Chalice, 1999.
Wink, Walter, ed. *Homosexuality and Christian Faith: Questions of Conscience for the Churches.* Minneapolis: Fortress, 1999.

# Bibliography

Augustine. "The Rule of St. Augustine." http://midwestaugustinians.org/roots-of-augustinian-spirituality/.

Bausch, William J. *A World of Stories for Preachers and Teachers (And All Who Love Stories That Move and Challenge)*. Mystic, CT: Twenty-Third Publications, 1999.

Bronski, Michael. "The Bridge to Manhood: A Gay Man Talks about Disappointing—and Loving—His Father." http://www.beliefnet.com/Love-Family/2004/06/The-Bridge-To-Manhood.aspx.

Brooten, Bernadette J. *Love Between Women: Early Christian Responses to Female Homoeroticism*. Chicago Series on Sexuality, History, and Society. Chicago: University of Chicago Press, 1996.

Brown, Peter. *The Body and Society: Men, Women, and Sexual Renunciation in Early Christianity*. New York: Columbia University Press, 1988.

Brownson, James V. *Bible, Gender, Sexuality: Reframing the Church's Debate on Same-Sex Relationships*. Grand Rapids: Eerdmans, 2013.

Caputo, John D. *What Would Jesus Deconstruct? The Good News of Postmodernism for the Church*. Church and Postmodern Culture. Grand Rapids: Baker Academic, 2007.

Carter, Warren G. *John and Empire: Initial Explorations*. London: T. & T. Clark, 2008.

Fee, Gordon. *The First Epistle to the Corinthians*. New International Commentary on the New Testament. Grand Rapids: Eerdmans, 1987.

Goss, Robert, and Mona West, eds. *Take Back the Word: A Queer Reading of the Bible*. Cleveland: Pilgrim, 2000.

Graff, E. J. *What Is Marriage For? The Strange Social History of Our Most Intimate Institution*. Boston: Beacon, 1999.

Hall, Douglas John. *Why Christian? For Those on the Edge of Faith*. Minneapolis: Fortress, 1998.

Heyward, Carter. *Touching Our Strength: The Erotic as Power and the Love of God*. New York: Harper & Row, 1989.

hooks, bell. *Feminist Theory: From Margin to Center*. Cambridge, MA: South End, 2000.

Hughes, Langston. "Mother to Son." In *Poems*, selected and edited by David Roessel, 24. New York: Knopf, 1999.

Josephus, Flavius. *The Antiquities of the Jews*. In *The Works of Flavius Josephus*. Translated by William Whiston. Auburn, NY: John E. Beardsley, 1895.

# Bibliography

King, Christopher. "A Love as Fierce as Death: Reclaiming the Song of Songs for Queer Lovers." In *Take Back the Word: A Queer Reading of the Bible*, edited by Robert Goss and Mona West, 126–42. Cleveland: Pilgrim, 2000.

Mbiti, John. *African Religions and Philosophy*. 2nd ed. Garden City, NY: Anchor, 1970.

McFague, Sallie. *Metaphorical Theology: Models of God in Religious Language*. Minneapolis: Fortress, 1982.

Philo of Alexandria. *On Abraham*. In *The Works of Philo Judaeus*. Translated by Charles Duke Yonge. http://www.earlychristianwritings.com/yonge/book22.html.

*Religion & Ethics NewsWeekly*. "Young Evangelical Christians and the 2008 Election." September 29, 2008. http://www.pbs.org/wnet/religionandethics/2008/09/29/survey-young-evangelical-christians-and-the-2008-election/866/.

Schiffman, Larry. *Texts and Traditions: A Source Reader for the Study of Second Temple and Rabbinic Judaism*. Hoboken, NJ: KTAV, 1998.

Schneiders, Sandra M. *Jesus Risen in Our Midst: Essays on the Resurrection of Jesus in the Fourth Gospel*. Collegeville, MN: Liturgical, 2013.

Stendahl, Krister. "Can Bishops Tell the Truth as They See It?" In *Christianity in the Twenty-First Century*, edited by Deborah A. Brown. New York: Crossroad, 2000.

Trible, Phyllis. *God and the Rhetoric of Sexuality*. Overtures to Biblical Theology. Philadelphia: Fortress, 1978.

Vines, Matthew. "The Gay Debate: The Bible and Homosexuality." http://www.matthewvines.com/transcript/.

Walker, Vaughn. "Perry v. Schwarzenegger." http://www.eqca.org/atf/cf/%7B34f258b3-8482-4943-91cb-08c4b0246a88%7D/WALKER%20PROP8DECISION.PDF.

Weems, Renita J. *What Matters Most: Ten Lessons in Living Passionately from the Song of Solomon*. West Bloomfield, MI: Walk Worthy, 2004.

Wilson, Ken. *A Letter to My Congregation: An Evangelical Pastor's Path to Embracing People Who Are Gay, Lesbian and Transgender in the Company of Jesus*. Canton, MI: David Crumm, 2014.

Witte, John, Jr. *From Sacrament to Contract: Marriage, Religion, and Law in the Western Tradition*. 1st ed. Family, Religion, and Culture. Louisville: Westminster John Knox, 1997.

www.ingramcontent.com/pod-product-compliance
Lightning Source LLC
Chambersburg PA
CBHW020848160426
43192CB00007B/838